RICHARDSON

"Mr. Richardson, reading the Manuscript of Sir Charles Grandison in 1751, to his Friends, in the Grotto of his House at North End, from a drawing made at the time by Miss Highmore"

1. Mr. Richardson in his usual morning dress
2. Mr. Mulso
3. Mr. Edward Mulso
4. Miss Mulso, afterwards Mrs. Chapone

5. Miss Prescott, afterwards Mrs. Mulso
6. The Revd. Mr. Duncombe
7. Miss Highmore, afterwards Mrs. Duncombe

(Reproduced by kind permission of the University Library, Cambridge)

RICHARDSON

by

BRIAN W. DOWNS

31328

NEW YORK

BARNES & NOBLE, INC.

Publishers · Booksellers · Since 1873

Published by
FRANK CASS AND COMPANY LIMITED
67 Great Russell Street, London WC1
by arrangement with Routledge & Kegan Paul, Ltd.

Published in the United States
in 1969
by Barnes & Noble, Inc.
105 Fifth Avenue, New York, N.Y. 10003

First edition   1928
New impression   1969

Printed in Great Britain

CONTENTS

SAMUEL RICHARDSON

Chapter One

THE LIFE

§ I

In the summer of 1757 Mr. Samuel Richardson, past master of the Stationers' Company in the city of London, received one of the handsomest of the compliments which had so deliciously bestrewed his amazing career. A gentleman from Leipzig—no doubt the prince of book-sellers, Philipp Erasmus Reich, who once made a special journey to kiss the inkpot from which Clarissa had risen like Aphrodite from the main—besought him to make a selection from his correspondence : translated and published, it would allow his German admirers to paint for themselves a portrait of the man whose own delineations had added so infinitely much to their knowledge of themselves and their fellow-men. To have his private letters published during his lifetime—such an honour had befallen none of the internationally accepted geniuses of his age, not Newton or Swift or that impious Monsieur de Voltaire who had done him the dubious favour of patronizing his chaste daughters, Pamela and Clarissa. Only Pope had seen his letters in print before he died, and that had nothing whatever to do with the humble requests of his friends. In fact, Erasmus furnished the only respectable precedent.

In a flutter of pleasure Richardson put the last touches to the volumes and files of his correspondents' letters, which he had kept carefully ordered and furnished with copies of his own replies : he scored through passages and whole letters unsuited for general reading, he toned down extravagant courtesies, he substituted dots and aliases for the proper names. Some of the revised papers he then referred back, for approbation, to those with whom they had been exchanged, reminding them that detection of their identity (if undesired) would be all the more improbable by a foreign public. Lady Bradshaigh, the most important of them, who two years before had vainly besought her friend to favour the world with his Autobiography or, alternatively, to countenance a Biography compiled by a syndicate of his intimates, strongly approved the German proposal, as well as the manner in which her own nine volumes of letters had been handled ; and there is neither evidence nor likelihood that others, consulted like her, proved unamenable. None the less, the project advanced no further. Perhaps the Weidmannsche Buchhandlung refused all risks during the Seven Years' War ; perhaps its energetic manager had not realized the magnitude of the undertaking when he first suggested it. Anyhow, neither during Richardson's life nor in the years immediately following his death, when his books were still living successes, were the letters which he had so carefully prepared for the press, put to it or even used as the basis of a Memoir, such as that which Arthur Murphy in 1762 prefixed to the first collection of Fielding's Works.

Not until 1804 was the gap filled, when, on the death of the novelist's last surviving child, his papers passed into the hands of the publisher, Richard Phillips, and Mrs. Barbauld edited for him *The Correspondence of Samuel Richardson . . . selected from the Original Manuscripts; bequeathed by him to his family.* This selection she prefaced by a valuable Biographical Account of 212 pages, derived partly from the materials she printed, partly from kindred documents which she omitted from the anthology, and partly from still current gossip and memories. A little was contributed to Mrs. Barbauld's account by biographical works published in the interval which had elapsed since her subject's death, such as Boswell's *Life of Johnson;* and rather more by the *Memoirs of the Life and Writings of Mr. Samuel Richardson,* attributed to his son-in-law Edward Bridgen, F.R.S., and printed in *The Universal Magazine* of January and February 1786. But Mrs. Barbauld's six octavo volumes constitute really the earliest source-book we have on Richardson's life—and also the last. Nothing of great importance is added to our knowledge of him by papers subsequently brought to light; of these the most important are a series of 150 letters between Richardson and Young, printed in *The Monthly Magazine* for December 1813 and subsequent issues.

Several of the correspondence-files on which Mrs. Barbauld had drawn (but by no means all) eventually passed, in whole or in part, into the hands of John Forster, the friend and biographer of Dickens; and he at his death left them to the Victoria and Albert Museum, South Kensington, where they fill nearly six folio volumes of about 150 letter-pages apiece.

In one respect this biographical material, for all its abundance, is defective and naturally so. Not until the reception of *Pamela* had, towards the end of 1740, made its author a person of consequence, did it occur to him to copy his private letters ; nor would, before this time, the recipients either preserve them or treasure up anecdotes concerning the writer. (A not very far-reaching exception to this generalization must be made for Aaron Hill. For the earliest letter between them, not at South Kensington, Mrs. Barbauld alleges the date 1730. She seems, however, to have made a slip in this, and the beginning of their correspondence and friendship should rather be dated at 6 March, 1735, when, in a letter of the Forster Collection which Mrs. Barbauld did not utilize, Aaron Hill addresses Richardson as a personal stranger. After that, it is true, there is a thin trickle of correspondence between the two.) From another point of view, however, the lack of documents from earlier years is no grave loss. Richardson's life after 1735 or 1740 is an uneventful one ; if but a fraction of what Jeffrey styled the melancholy farrago of his letters had come down, posterity could still compose pretty much the same biography and mental image of him in his successful maturity as it can now ; and there is little reason to suppose that the records of his youth and early middle age would yield excitements such as are altogether lacking from the annals with which we are familiar.

§ 2

Some material facts, however, remain undeniably obscure. The first of these concerns the time and place of his birth. No documents or other incontrovertible evidence bearing on this event have hitherto come to light. Posterity, then, has no choice but to accept the statements, vague and uncorroborated as they are, of his son-in-law, that he was born in 1689, and of himself,

4

that he was born in Derbyshire. There is some slight probability that the date may be narrowed down between the limits of 1 January and 4 July 1689.

But the mystery, trifling as it is, which envelopes the details of his arrival into the world, extends rather more perplexingly to the remoter circumstances of it. On these he vouchsafed some information to the Dutch translator of *Clarissa* and *Grandison* :

" My father's business was that of a joiner, [*i.e.*, a cabinet-maker] . . . He was a good draughtsman, and understood architecture. His skill and ingenuity, and an understanding superior to his business, with his remarkable integrity of heart and manners, made him personally beloved by several persons of rank, among whom were the Duke of Monmouth and the first Earl of Shaftsbury, both so noted in our English history ; their known favour for him having, on the Duke's attempt on the crown, subjected him to be looked upon with a jealous eye, notwithstanding he was noted for a quiet and inoffensive man, he thought proper, on the decollation of the first-named unhappy nobleman, to quit his London business, and to retire to Derbyshire, though to his great detriment ; and there I, and three other children out of nine, were born."

The strangest thing about this somewhat surprising and elaborate statement, is its failure to square with the only well-authenticated fact relative to this period, advanced, together with much other interesting material, in recent years by Mr. A. L. Reade : namely, that as late as the spring of 1687, more than eighteen months after the Duke of Monmouth's decollation, Samuel Richardson the elder (the father of the future novelist) and his wife had a daughter baptized in the parish of their domicile, St. Botolph's, Aldersgate Street, London. Something evidently befell old Mr. Richardson during the reign of James II which somehow redounded to his discredit ; what it was has never been established ; and the son's account may well be nothing more than one of the mystifications in which he was by no means averse to indulging when moral and material profit might ensue.

Moreover, it appears by no means certain that the pacification of the country after the accession of William and Mary in the year commonly assigned to Richardson's birth entailed the return of his parent to their home. It is indeed more likely than not that his youth was passed out of London and that he received all the education he ever had at a " private grammar school in the country," which has been inconclusively identified with that of Smalley. Certainly the pretensions of Christ's Hospital and the London Merchant Taylors' School to enrol him among their past members have never been satisfactorily supported. Wherever he received it, the novelist's formal education cannot have amounted to much more than the proverbial three R's. Anne Richardson, his youngest daughter, claimed to remember her father talking Latin with Edward Young ; but it seems more probable to suppose with Mrs. Barbauld that he forgot from disuse any which his school may have taught him and that the latinity put into the mouth of Mr. Brand in *Clarissa* was furnished by his friend, Mr. J. Channing.

§ 3

Samuel Richardson the elder (*ca.* 1651 —*ca.* 1730)

claimed descent from gentry indigenous near Byfleet in Surrey, who had on one occasion under James I filled the Speaker's chair ; the family of his wife, Elizabeth Lane (*ca.* 1650 —*ca.* 1736), whom he had married at St. Botolph's Aldersgate on 7 January 1675, was also described by her son as " not ungenteel." It is then not outside the realm of probability that such parents should as their later descendants reported, consider the Church a suitable profession for a lad whom his playmates nick-named Gravity and Serious and who at the tender age of ten or less had taken upon himself the mission of rebuking a widow five times his age for her back-biting ways. When young Samuel's elementary schooling was com-pleted, however, funds were insufficient for the reali-zation of so lofty an ambition ; but he was allowed to choose the craft, since craft it must be, to which to be apprenticed. He selected that of printer, since it would, as he believed, afford him more opportunities than any other for reading and the consequent improvement of his mind.

On 1 July, 1706, then, as the Stationers' Register records, he was " bound to John Wilde for seven years." This John Wilde was a neighbour and, we may believe, a friend of the Richardson family, owning, in the words of a contemporary " a very noble Printing-house in Aldersgate-Street." Though apparently an unpleasant master, he managed to retain his apprentice after he was out of his indentures in 1713, and Samuel Richardson stayed on with him, as corrector and overseer, in fact (to quote his later boast) as " the pillar of his house." The reason for his continuance in Aldersgate Street may perhaps be found in the *beaux yeux* of the old man's daughter Martha, a girl just eight years old when he

7

entered the house. At all events, after John Wilde's death he married her, in Charterhouse Chapel, on 23 November, 1721.

Meanwhile, on 13 June, 1715, Richardson had taken up the freedom of the Stationers' Company and, three or four years later, established himself on his own account, in an unidentified court off Fleet Street. Of his earliest activities as a master-printer we know as good as nothing. The early accounts tell of a gentleman, greatly his superior in degree and of ample fortune, who, had he lived, intended high things for him and who " was a master of the epistolary style," which he exercised in a copious correspondence with his young protégé ; but whether he made the acquaitance of Richardson as a customer is unknown ; possibly he was a legacy of the old days when the elder Samuel in his turn had been a *persona grata* with gentlemen greatly his superior in degree and had suffered on their account. There also survives from this time the equally unsubstantial rumour of a connexion between the printer and Philip, Duke of Wharton. Richardson is said to have been the first printer of *The True Briton*, a weekly begun by Wharton in June, 1723, and to have written the letter signed " A.B.", which takes up almost the whole of No. 6 (dated 21 June, 1723). That letter voiced opinions so directly opposed to the general trend of the paper's propaganda, that it is not surprising to learn of his immediate supersession in the printing. About this time, or early in 1724, Richardson removed to Salisbury Court (now Salisbury Square), Fleet Street, which had evidently lost the unsavoury reputation attached to it by *The London Spy* a quarter of a century earlier. Mrs. Pilkington described the premises in her *Memoirs* as of " a very grand outward Appearance " and

8

certainly they were large enough to accommodate his very extensive business for thirty years. Samuel Richardson had made a prosperous start in life.

Since eighteenth-century printers did not, as a general custom, divulge their names on the books which issued from their presses, the typographical history of that age is hard to chronicle ; and, in view of the fact that Richardson's business was great enough to warrant a pay-roll of between £30 and £40 a week in 1756, we know uncommonly little about his professional activities. But it is a matter of some importance to prosecute enquiry into them, as they afford the likeliest of the scanty clues to his own reading. The author of the Memoir in *The Universal Magazine* gave some slight attention to the matter, making him responsible for the printing of the first edition of the *Journals* of the House of Commons (to which he had been appointed printer on 24 January, 1738), as well as of *The Daily Journal* in 1736 and 1737 and *The Daily Gazetteer* in 1738. Unhappily, some of this information is palpably incorrect ; for, according to the statement found in each copy, *The Daily Journal* was printed between 1 January, 1736 and 8 May, 1737 by T. Cooper. There is nothing to say for or against the statement as it applies to the rest of the newspaper-printing. The *Journals* of the House of Commons certainly came from his press. The *Memoir* alleges too that Richardson was concerned with the printing of James Mauclerc's *Christian Magazine* (1748), a periodical it has been impossible to consult. Nichols gives a short list including Volume II of de Thou's *Historiarum sui temporis. . . . Libri CXXXVIII* (1733) and Dr. William Webster's *Weekly Miscellany*, which can, however, only have come from Richardson's press (if at all) during the last fifteen

months of its career, between March 1740 and June 1741 ;
to these he adds the two publications of the Society for the
Encouragement of Learning, to which further reference
will shortly be made. These meagre lists of the early
authorities may be supplemented by the following :
Richardson's own works ; volumes V and VI of *A Collection of Voyages and Travels* (1732) made by Awnsham
Churchill ; Patrick Delany's *Life of David* (1740) and
probably his *Reflections upon Polygamy* (1738) as well ;
Alzira and almost certainly some others of Aaron Hill's
works ; John Conybeare's *Sermons* (1757) ; the second
part of Young's *Night Thoughts* (1742) and a one-volume
re-issue of the whole in 1749 ; his *Argument drawn from
the Circumstance of Christ's Death* (1758) ; the *Modern
Part* of the *Universal History* by Smollett and others, at any
rate in part ; *The Histories of Some of the Penitents in the
Magdalen-house* (1760) ; and Elizabeth Carter's translation of *Epictetus* (*n.d.*), the printing bill for six hundred
and fifty copies of which, as we happen to know, amounted
to £67 7s. od. Mr. Septimus Rivington states that he
was printer to the Lord Mayor and did an extensive
business in so-called " trade " books also. As Richardson
seems to have known of its contents before publication,
it is probable too that he printed Smollett's *Peregrine
Pickle* (1751) ; and there are some grounds for thinking
that he printed *The Plain Dealer* on its first appearance,
periodically, in 1724 and 1725 : he certainly published
the reprint of 1730, and from the advertisements in the
original edition it seems that he had dabbled in publication
before—as, on the appearance of his own books and of the
Universal History, he was to do later—and had been
responsible for the issue of Michael de Castelnau's *Memoirs
of the Reign of Francis II and Charles IX of France* (1725).

It is not improbable that he combined the calling of bookseller and perhaps even library-keeper with those of printer and publisher ; a few rather obscure, though quite unimportant passages in his letters would give support to such a theory. On the professional merits of Richardson it is impossible for a layman to pronounce ; Mr. W. B. Thorne, who contributed a specialist paper on the subject to the *Library*, declared that "his work seems to have been carefully executed ; " certainly the fly-sheet setting forth *The Case of Samuel Richardson, Printer* (almost certainly his own work) and the *Negotiations of Sir Thomas Roe*, a vast folio, look equally handsome specimens of typography.

§ 4

On 23 January, 1731, in a distressful period which cost him the lives of eleven near connections within two years, his wife, who had borne him six short-lived children, died at the age of thirty-two. Not long afterwards, at a time and place unknown, he married again. His second wife, the Mrs. Richardson of his famous years, was also the daughter of a printer in the parish of St. Botolph's, Aldersgate Street. This lady, Elizabeth Leake (1697-1773), had for brother James Leake, "the illustrious Leake of Bath" as Lord Orrery calls him, one of the most eminent of English booksellers. To his Bett Richardson generally alluded with a certain tempered affection and condescension. " My wife is a very worthy Woman," he wrote to another lady. She suffered all her life from low spirits and, since she refused to go calling

and in any way cut a figure, evidently felt ill at ease in the
more exalted company her husband kept in the last twenty
years of their married life.   She had a failing inherited
by her daughters, " Love of Bed on Mornings," particularly annoying to a husband who rose at 5 a.m. and required
less than six hours' sleep himself ; and he could remark
with a spice of heart-felt bitterness quite foreign to his
nature : " the Man who has passed all his Days single, is
not always and in every thing a Loser."   The second
Mrs. Richardson likewise produced six children ; but of
these only two, the solitary son included, died young ; the
rest survived their father and some of them have many
descendants alive to-day.   They were : Mary Richardson
(1734 or 1735-1783), who, after two other offers, married
Mr. Ditcher, a Bath surgeon in 1757 ; Martha Richardson (1736-85), her father's favourite amanuensis, who
became Mrs. Edward Bridgen ; Sarah Richardson (1740-
73), who also married a doctor, Crowther by name ; and
Anne Richardson (born 1737), who died a spinster in 1803.

§ 5

In 1735, on entering into relations with Aaron Hill,
Richardson begins to emerge from the penumbra mirrored in the conjectures and hesitations of his biographers.
He was by now a man of substance.   In 1738—as an
instance of this—he started renting from Mr. John Smith,
junior, the north half of a fine house at North-End near
the Hammersmith Turnpike Road, which had been
occupied before him by " one Sherwood, an Attorney "
and by the eccentric relict of Lord Ranelagh, who, finding
the rent of this house too low for her gentility, got an

obliging landlord to raise it to a decent figure. To increase its amenities Richardson took on some adjacent open land for £5 *per annum*. Whether he installed or found already *in situ* an " alcove " in the garden does not appear ; but it became most closely associated with him and perhaps the distinguishing feature of the place, was removed from it when he did and was celebrated in Dodsley's *Collection of Poems by Several Hands;* for

> " Here the soul-harrowing genius form'd
> His PAMELA'S enchanting story !
> And here divine CLARISSA died
> A martyr to our sex's glory."

(Another poet is found referring to it as an
" awful Cell
Where sober Contemplation loves to dwell.")

To "*agreeable surburbane* North End" with its grotto or garden-house Richardson would retreat every week-end, and, in normal times, when business in town did not press too heavily, for a further night or two during the week. He kept it constantly open, most suitable for inviting friends to spend long periods of time in semi-independence—whole seasons if they chose. The house still stands in the North End Road, Fulham ; it is now called "The Grange" and numbered 111. Burne-Jones inhabited it during the last thirty-one years of his life, and Mr. Fairfax Murray after him. It is probable that it did not represent Richardson's first experiment in week-end villas ; an unidentified Corney House, from which an early letter is dated, may have served in that capacity.

Richardson had clearly become a warm man.[1] But not only that : he had also acquired, among his fellow-printers and other members of the book-trade at any rate, some literary reputation as well. " He did," says Mrs. Barbauld, " a good deal of business for the booksellers, in writing for them indexes, prefaces, and, as he stiles them, honest dedications." When, in 1736, the historian Carte founded a Society for the Encouragement of Learning, he became a member and was duly appointed one of its three printers. In that capacity he turned out—and most nobly too—two among the ten pieces of learning which the society encouraged, a reprint of Alexander Stuart's *Dissertatio de Structura et Motu Musculari* (1738) and the first volume of *The Negotiations of Sir Thomas Roe in his Embassy to the Ottoman Porte from the Year* 1621 *to* 1628 *Inclusive.* . . . *Now first published from the Originals* (1740). The latter work was edited by Carte, but the dedication to King George II was signed (and presumably written) by Richardson, and the elaborate Tables of Contents and Index look like work in which he would have revelled, though it cannot be proved his. Similarly, he had, according to a later edition of this work, a part in bringing De Foe's *Tour Thro' the Whole Island of Great Britain* up to date for the second edition of 1738 and again for the third in 1742 ; and he brought out an edition of Æsop's *Fables,* no doubt that published by Osborn " with instructive Morals and Reflections, abstracted from all Party Considerations . . . Containing 240 Fables, with a Cut Ingraved on Copper to each Fable, And the Life of Æsop prefixed " (1740).

[1] It seems impossible to assess income and wealth except from his easy style of living and the certainty that he could afford it. Knowledge of isolated transactions, such as seventy guineas for the Irish copyright of *Clarissa*, is almost useless for the purpose.

§ 6

But his reputation for Superiority, which had helped to make him printer to the Society for the Encouragement of Learning, was to prove more momentous in the history of civilization. Two of his friends in the book-trade, John Osborn, "a very honest and punctual Acquaintance," and Charles Rivington, the founder of the celebrated publishing firm of that name as well as a fellow-enthusiast for the Encouragement of Learning, tempted him to venture just a little out of the shallow depths in which so far he had been content to exercise his literary talents. In his own words, they

" . . . entreated me to write for them a little volume of Letters, in a common style, on such subjects as might be of use to those country readers, who were unable to indite for themselves."

That is to say, they wanted to reap their share of the substantial harvest with which " Polite Letter-Writers " of various sorts had enriched enterprising publishers since the days of Queen Elizabeth. But Richardson wished to elevate this humbre *genre* :

" Will it be any harm, said I, in a piece you want to be written so low, if we should instruct them how they should think and act in common cases, as well as indite ? They were the more urgent with me to begin the little volume for this hint."

Richardson set about it and ultimately produced the

desired volume, which Rivington and Osborn, in conjunction with the author's Bath brother-in-law, published in January, 1741, at the price of two-and-six.

In a prefatory Note the author enlarges a little further on his general design and method, which he sums up as "NATURE, PROPRIETY of CHARACTER, PLAIN SENSE, and GENERAL USE ; " he aims everywhere to " write to the *Judgment*, rather than to the *Imagination*" and his model letters endeavour "to inculcate the Principles of *Virtue* and *Benevolence* ; to describe *properly*, and recommend *strongly*, the SOCIAL and RELATIVE DUTIES." After these protestations follow the 173 Familiar Letters which do what the title-page promises—Directing not only the Requisite Style and Forms To Be Observed in Writing Familiar Letters ; But How to Think and Act Justly and Prudently in the Common Concerns of Human Life. Their main purpose is to provide formulæ for, among other things, *A threatening Letter from a Steward on Delay of Payment*, for *Recommending a Wet-Nurse*, and for condoling with *A Widow on the Death of her Husband*, on which the author judiciously observes in a foot-note that, with small variations, the same Arguments may be used to a Husband on the Death of his Wife, and on other melancholy Occasions of the like Nature.

There is something rather puritanical about the whole collection. The people whom Richardson meant to help would, it seems, not readily put pen to paper except on some unpleasant occasion, in order to condole, to warn, to dissuade or to beseech. " To Think and Act Justly and Prudently " generally results in writing in a carping or minatory strain. One " tenderly affectionate Father", expostulates with his Tom for starting to keep a Horse too early (Letter XI), another " most indulgent Father " writes to his son to " dissuade him from the Vice of Drinking to Excess " (Letter XXXVI), the subject being pursued in Letter XXXVII. In another place the country readers could note the expressions employed by " a Son reduced by his own Extravagance, requesting his Father's Advice, on his Intention to turn Player [*i.e.* Actor]," and the prompt " Father's Answer, setting forth the Inconveniences and Disgrace attending the Profession of a Player " (XLVII and XLVIII). Nor are women spared. Letter LXIII is addressed " To a Daughter in a Country Town, who encourages the Address of a Subaltern "—A Case, the compiler adds in brackets, too frequent in Country Towns.

Richardson, however, essays a lighter vein also, as in *A humorous Epistle of neighbourly Occurrences and News to a Bottle-Companion abroad.* (LXXVI). But his humour has a somewhat macabre tang. Dear Bob's old Bottle-Companion, and humble Servant begins his detailed chronicle with : " I have had the Misfortune to lose my Son *Jo*," but then waxes more dégagé : " *Jack Kid* of the *Fountain*, where we kept our Club, has lost his Wife, who was a special Bar-Keeper, got his Maid *Prisc.* with Child—you remember the Slut, by her mincing Airs—marry'd her, and is broke : But not till he had with his horrid Stum, poison'd half the Society . . . for, truly, *Bob*, we began to tumble like rotten Sheep . . . first, honest laughing *Jack Adams* kick'd up of a Fever *Tom Dandy* fell into a Jaundice and Dropsy . . . *Roger Harman*, the Punster, then tipt off the Perch, after very little Warning ; And was followed in a Week by *Arthur Sykes*." After a prolonged catalogue of death and disease we read that " *Joshua Williams* the Cheesemonger, a strange projecting Fellow, you know ! is carried out of his Shop into a Sponging-house by *his own Maggots*." Almost the only cheerful news which Bob's friend has to retail is that "old clumsy Parson *Dromedary* is made a Dean, and has Hopes, by his Sister's means, who is a Favourite of a certain great Man, to be a Bishop."

Sometimes, it is worth observing, a series of letters is connected by some common tie, and intrinsically the most valuable letters in the collection form a group of this kind (CXLIX-CLIX), entitled *From a Young Lady in Town to her Aunt in the Country*, in which the writer gives accounts of what were then esteemed the sights of London : the Tower, the Monument, St. Paul's, Westminster Hall, Chelsea Hospital, Kensington Palace, Greenwich Park (reached by water), Bethlehem Hospital, Vauxhall, Westminster Abbey. She winds up with a concert and two plays, all of which incurred the young lady's censure : she could not away with the new fashion of Recitative to which the concert introduced her, *Hamlet* was spoiled for her by the Harlequinade which followed, and in the Comedy " the Parts acted by Women had several Speeches that I thought not quite consistent with the Modesty of the Sex. . . . Nor did I perceive, that so many Expressions, which are oftener miscalled *arch*, than more truly named *obscene*, were put into the Mouths of the Men as of the Women." But she consoled herself by noting that the " utmost Decency was observed " by the audience and that several of the women (so she was assured) " who get their Bread upon the Stage, are strictly virtuous."

Rather more ambitious and interesting from the artistic point of view are the first six letters of the series. They are represented as the writing of four different correspondents, and from their communications we can piece together a complete story of a high-spirited young man, William, not deemed clever enough for the Bar and so articled to a trade, growing obstreperous after the death of his father and settling down to sobriety on discovering and being forced to disclose a fraud perpetrated by a fellow-apprentice upon their master. Similarly, Letters XV to XXI, taken in conjunction, tell a love-story.

§ 7

It was while he was engaged on the *Familiar Letters* that Richardson received a two-fold impulse to write his first celebrated and "original" work, *Pamela*. The successful experiment of making an organic whole from six or seven letters cannot but have suggested to him the idea of a more elaborate structure, in which a vaster correspondence should convey a longer and more complex sequence of events. And, more specifically, just as Letter XXXI, recommending Mr. John Andrews as a superior Man-Servant, gave him the surname for his heroine, so Letter CXXXVIII (*A Father to a Daughter in Service on Hearing her Master's Attempting her Virtue*) indicated the kind of story that might be told about her in this way and reminded him of some happenings which he had long considered suitable for literary treatment.

Nearly one hundred years later an almost unknown writer, Charles Dickens, with a publisher's contract in his pocket, "thought of Mr. Pickwick" and immediately found his imagination flooded with incidents, turns of phrase and personages ; in the same way it would seem that Richardson "thought" of the story of *Pamela* and straightway became quasi-demoniacally possessed by it. That expression may sound somewhat strong to use for our methodical printer, now past the fiftieth year of his age and the enemy of all frenzies, fine or fierce ; but the facts seem to warrant it.   On the 10 November, 1739, as the routine of his printing-house made him write on the manuscript, he put aside the papers of the *Familiar Letters* and settled to his new theme ; and in two months to the day, on 10 January 1740, the novel stood complete— though, perhaps, as Fräulein Danielowski has plausibly suggested, not in the full and final form represented by the first edition, since that did not appear until 8 November of that same year 1740.   No author's—or even "editor's "—name appeared on the two duodecimo volumes, which were sold at six shillings the set.

Pamela proved immensely successful ; edition followed edition ; so did worry.   Already in April 1741, before the third edition was exhausted, Richardson received information of a notorious Invasion of his Plan.   One Kelly, "a Bookseller's Hackney," (whom Austin Dobson tentatively identified with John Kelly, the author of the *Universal Spectator*) had been commissioned by the bookseller Chandler to write a sequel to the book of the year.   As nothing short of an unworthy compromise with them could deter Chandler and Kelly from their project, Richardson felt himself obliged to take as much of the wind out of their sails as he could by writing a sequel of his own and advertising the fact as soon as negotiations with the pirates had broken down.   The bastard *Pamela's Conduct in High Life* duly appeared in September 1741.   But Richardson had toiled all the summer at his forced labour so energetically that his own *Pamela in her Exalted Condition* (now often called *Pamela, Part II*) could appear before the year was out with the same publishers as the first two volumes, *i.e.* Richardson himself

and his two friends, Rivington and Osborn. Further
pirates superadded vexation of another sort. In spite of
his care to prevent such a leakage, dishonest employees
of Richardson's smuggled sheets of *Pamela II* out of his
printing-house to Ireland, where the Dublin bookseller,
George Faulkner, issued an edition of his own. This
was doubly annoying, as the author not only received no
benefit from it in the shape of Irish royalties, but had to
sustain its competition with his own venture in more or
less neutral markets, such as the Scottish. He and his
partners promptly retaliated by obtaining a patent from
the Crown, granting them from 13 January, 1742, a
fourteen years' monopoly in *Pamela* throughout George
II's kingdoms and dominions, but, in the chaotic condition of copyright at that time, it probably availed them
little against determined rogues like Chandler and
Faulkner.

§ 8

To adopt literature as a calling in the 1740's meant
ranking with Grub Street. So it never occurred to
Richardson to sell up his business, retire to Fulham and
turn professional man of letters or, as his modern counterpart would do, to go on more extensive travel than his
annual " Toure " of two to three weeks in South England.
As far as can be seen from this distance of time, his activities as a writer affected but little the day-to-day routine
hardened by twenty years of life as a City printer.
Neither, Pamela once married, does he appear very
seriously or urgently to have considered the career of a successor to her. The goad of Kelly drove him another
stage on his predestined road, yet involuntarily, reluctantly.

But ink is one of those insidious drugs that set up a "habit." So by June, 1744, we find *The Lady's Legacy* well advanced, at any rate in rough draft, and about the same time a "wide and arduous plan" of the whole sent to Aaron Hill. By October, 1746, *Clarissa*, as *The Lady's Legacy* was finally called, seems to have been virtually complete, though by then the author may not have begun the labours he did undertake at some time of reducing its great bulk to more usual proportions. On 1 December, 1747, the first two volumes were published by the author in conjunction with A. Millar, John Osborn, John and James Rivington, and James Leake ; on 26 April, 1748, volumes III and IV ; and on 6 December, 1748, the last three—making seven in all.

§ 9

After the publication of *Clarissa*, Richardson, apprehending " he should be obliged to stop, by reason of his precarious state of health, and a variety of avocation which claimed his first attention," again allowed himself the same sort of rest as after *Pamela II* ; and for two and a half years there is no mention of literary activities in the surviving correspondence. During this interval, however, he busied himself with several literary odds and ends, among them his best known minor work. He issued the *Meditations from the Sacred Books*, to which the heroine of *Clarissa* had been stated to have recourse, though apparently he had made the compilation at first rather for the sake of what might be called artistic veracity than for publication. For the third and fourth editions of *Clarissa* (which appeared simultaneously in 1751) he established the definitive text, rather less than ten per cent. longer than that of the first edition, and compiled his " Collection of such of the Moral and Instructive Sentiments interspersed throughout that work, as may be presumed to be of *general* Use and Service." And on 19 February, 1751, there appeared his solitary contribution to *The Rambler*, a twice-weekly periodical edited (and mostly written) by Samuel Johnson, who proclaimed in his grandest chest-notes : " The reader is indebted for this day's entertainment to an author from whom the age has received greater favours, who has enlarged the knowledge of human nature, and taught the passions to move at the command of virtue." The entertainment, summarized in the Table of Contents as " Advice to unmarried ladies," consisted of a contrast between the modest behaviour of young women in the writer's youth and their tireless gadding after pleasure characteristic of the time of writing; it ended with the customary and essentially hypocritical lament that the gay coquette of to-day " has companions indeed, but no lovers,"—fails (that is to say) of her conscious or unconscious purpose in the world,—and with a request to " The Rambler " himself to expatiate further on the same text. This diatribe, with which no doubt Noah regaled his daughters-in-law in the Ark and which some congregation or other hears every Sunday from Christmas to Advent, had the usual effect. A number of defenceless girls were bored (without being reformed), while *The Rambler*, for the only time in its short life, really sold well. So, at any rate, Chalmers maintains.

§ 10

By the time that No. 97 of *The Rambler* appeared, the story of *Sir Charles Grandison* must have been taking

shape in the writer's mind. About the genesis of this
work we have indeed more information than usual. In
a letter of 16 December, 1749, Lady Bradshaigh refers,
in terms that suggest a familiar subject, to a projected
book about "a good man . . . a man who needs no
repentance." On 21 January, 1751, over a year later,
Richardson could, however, still write rather peevishly
to M. Dufreval : " I am teazed by a dozen ladies of note
and of virtue, to give them a good man, as they say I have
been partial to their sex, and unkind to my own. But,
Sir, my nervous infirmities you know—time mends them
not—and Clarissa has almost killed me. You know how
my business engages me. . . ." This would seem to
suggest that the idea of the dozen ladies had hardly kindled
yet, but three days later we find Thomas Edwards men-
tioning the heroine Harriet Byron by name, and on
8 May he writes again that he is " exceedingly glad to
hear that you have found your Good Man, for I was
informed from Rochester some time ago that Miss Harriet
was very much grown ; which made me hope that she was
almost ready for him." But the work made no spectacular
progress. On 17 November, 1751, Mrs. Delany con-
fided to Mrs. Dewes : " I fear it will be a long time, if
ever, before Mr. Richardson's ' good man ' is produced,
and I am afraid his health will suffer for his too close
attention to it ; he has undertaken a *very hard task*, which
is to please the gay and the good, but Mrs. D[onnellan ?]
says, as far as he has gone he has succeeded wonderfully."
All the time, however, even if long uncertain about his
hero and unable to " find " him, Richardson was persever-
ing with that coral-like industry of his. A fire at his
City establishment in the early autumn of 1752, which
destroyed many of his papers, evidently did not touch the

24

new manuscript. For by 25 October he was able to report the completion of the first draft. By the beginning of August, 1753, after the usual exhausting revision, in which the author felt compelled to scratch out more than a fifth of the whole, Volumes I and II were set up in type. It was proposed to issue two volumes at a time with fair intervals between each batch ; but embarrassments arose, necessitating the publication of the first four volumes in November 1753, Volumes V and VI the next month, and the seventh (and last) volume in March 1754.

The embarrassments were once more the work of Irish pirates, against whom Richardson had taken special care to safeguard himself. On the old principle that the greatest thief proved the most effective thief-taker, he had entrusted the Dublin edition of *Clarissa* to none other than George Faulkner and had received seventy guineas from him as consideration. On the same terms he again arranged to send him sheets of *Sir Charles Grandison* as they were printed, so that, from them, the book might be set up anew in Ireland—such a procedure, in accordance with the customs of the Irish book-trade, assuring to him or his agent the Irish copyright. And to make the kind of leakage by which *Pamela II* was conveyed to Ireland more unlikely, he had various parts of the new book printed in three different printing-houses and then stored in a separate warehouse under the charge of one Peter Bishop. Peter Bishop, however, if you accept the plausible accusation levelled against him in *The Case of Samuel Richardson* (a flysheet, consisting of three pages and dated 14 September, 1753), played him false and allowed sheets to pass over to Ireland. There a syndicate composed of John Exshaw, Henry Saunders and Peter Wilson reprinted them and announced not merely speedy publication of the book, but their intention to be the first in the field for acquiring the Scottish rights and those of translation into French. Faulkner, realizing the failure of his original scheme, in pursuance of " an established, invariable and constant custom among the Booksellers of Dublin," prudently obtained a fifth share in the piratical syndicate by letting the others have access to his own (corrected) sheets and then had the impudence to cut down his responsibility for the covenanted consideration money from seventy guineas to fourteen, leaving his accomplices to owe the balance. Richardson was very angry, and rightly so, but had no legal redress and could not, as he hoped to do through Lord Orrery, bring political influence to bear on his " case."   All he could do was to set out all the wrongs the Irish book-market had inflicted on him in *An Address to the Public*, dated 1 February, 1754. Economico-literary relations between all the various English-speaking communities at that time somewhat resembled those still obtaining between Great Britain and the United States of America. For "at present," Richardson remarked in his flysheet, " the *English Writers* may be said, from the Attempts and Practices of the *Irish* Booksellers and Printers, to live in an Age of *Liberty* but not of *Property*."

It may be noted in passing that on this occasion Richardson for the first time avowed in public his authorship of the three novels.

§ 11

Richardson was sixty-five years of age, or very nearly, when the last volume of *Grandison* appeared : the work on it and the unforeseen worries attending its publication had much shaken him and his health seemed finally ruined. It had never been robust, for three not altogether incompatible reasons, which he used to advance alternatively, as occasion demanded : *viz*, extreme application to work in his youth, the shock of losing so many near and dear relations, especially in 1730 and 1731, and repletion. Whatever the cause and exact nature of his complaints—which manifested themselves chiefly in nervous affections, such as " wicked sleeplessness," extreme sensitiveness to impressions, hatred of crowds, dizziness, mistiness before the eyes, startings, tremblings of the legs and of the hands, which for days together would prevent his holding a pen—Richardson applied every possible remedy to extirpate them. " Five times, at least," he boasted somewhat mournfully, " I have been through ye whole Physical Circle." He went about with Hartshorn and Palsie-Drops, his pockets a little apothecary's shop. He turned vegetarian and teetotaller ; he drank the tar-water so greatly in vogue at his time, and, if he did not try port wine laced with sage tea, it was not because that drench had not been recommended to him. Lastly, with great assiduity, he rode upon the Chamber-Horse, a liver-shaking device now only known to Swedish gymnasts and ocean-travellers.

It seemed then in March 1754 that the tale of his literary works was all but told. Of course, he was at once beset again by the same people or the same sort of people who had five years before urged him to furnish the Virtuous Lady with a pendant in the shape of an Impeccable Gentleman. Lady Echlin desired him to complete the series Virtuous Maid (*Pamela*), Virtuous *Demi-Vierge* (*Clarissa*), Virtuous Wife (*Grandison*) . . . with

a new book about a Virtuous Widow ; her sister, Lady
Bradshaigh, went one better and adumbrated a tale revolving round *two* widows, one the relict of a good, the other
of a bad husband ; Lady Bradshaigh further suggested
some volumes of Miscellanies and, as has been said, an
Autobiography ; another friend called for the Life and
Death of a Female Dram-Taker, a *Gin Alley* in High
Life, so to speak. In this place should be mentioned the
rather obscure affair of Hortensia Beaumont, a minor
character in *Sir Charles Grandison*. At the end of the
fifth Volume of the *Correspondence* which she edited
Mrs. Barbauld printed a *History of Mrs. Beaumont, a
Fragment, in a letter from Dr. Bartlett to Miss Byron*, and
in *The London Mercury* for February 1923 Mr. Iolo
Williams announced that a packet of papers to which he
had access contained four further letters " centring round "
the same character. The tale is that to which Thomas
Edwards referred when, on 4 February, 1755, he wrote
to Richardson that " Mrs. Beaumont's story would, from
what I have seen of it, be both entertaining and
instructive ; but after what we have been favoured with,
would, I doubt, seem uninteresting." It seems more
likely that these fragments were left over as superfluous
after the last revision of *Grandison* and taken up again
with a view to further development than that they were,
in 1755, fresh compositions, designed as the beginning of
a new work. For Richardson made it quite clear, as his
labour on *Sir Charles Grandison* drew to a conclusion and
his Averseness to the Pen grew upon him, that this was
his last truly original work. All he wanted to do thereafter, in the realm of literature at least, was to compile
*A Collection of the Sentiments, Maxims, Cautions, and
Reflexions, Contained in Pamela, Clarissa, and Sir Charles*

Grandison (duly published in 1755) and to subject *Pamela* to a drastic revision—a project which was never realized. To those then who plied him with their inspirations for new works, he would suggest some co-operative venture in the epistolary manner, in which he could really and truly confine himself to the part of " Editor," or slyly answer that he might think of the next *opus* when all the beauties and subtleties of the earlier work had been appreciated.

But he could not—or, at any rate, as we have seen, did not—" retire " from literature completely. He may, as the title-page of that work boasts, have looked through and suggested improvements for *The History of Sir William Harrington*, first published in 1771 as " written some years since, And revised and corrected By the late Mr. Richardson," though Mrs. Richardson publicly disavowed any connexion. All that, in his ignorance of French, he could do for the English translation of Mademoiselle de Lussan's semi-historical *Vie de L. Balbe-Berton de Crillion*, which also claimed his co-operation, was to advise " some Notes of the Massacre of Paris, and Assassination of Henry IV ; Cotemporary Transactions." The elaborate index to the book calls to mind his handiwork in *The Negotiations of Sir Thomas Roe*. His literary end, indeed, strangely resembled his humble beginnings.

§ 12

Nor, for all his fame and years and prosperity, did he retire from business—though we find him in 1755 planning to entrust an increasing proportion of it to a nephew and on 24 June, 1760, taking into partnership Catherine Lintot, the daughter of Pope's publisher Henry Lintot.

SAMUEL RICHARDSON

In 1754—a great year for the Stationers, since in it they supplied the city of London with its Lord Mayor—Richardson was appointed master of their company, "a position," it is said, "as lucrative as it was honourable." Late in the following year, at a cost of £1,400, he moved his printing-works into new, large premises in White Lion Court, which led out of Salisbury Court, "97 Feet long one Range, 60 Feet the other," as he wrote to Lady Bradshaigh, "joined together by a kind of Bridge thrown over a tolerably paved Passage of about 12 Feet wide . . . I *must* remove from the handsome and roomy House I live in, to a House less handsome and less roomy : but infinitely more convenient, it adjoining to, and as I have managed it, opening into the paved Court that separates my double-winged Building, and, at the same time, giving me a very convenient Passage into Fleet-Street." He continued to print the Journals of the House of Commons and in 1760, with his new partner, obtained the rights to print Law Patents, which Henry Lintot had held from 1748 to his death in 1758.

On 28 May, 1761, Miss Talbot, the adopted daughter of the Archbishop of Canterbury, saw him and reported him, though very trembly, melancholy and bad-tempered as looking "so well." But there are indications that the final decline had clearly set in by then. His fairly extensive correspondence does not seem to have been maintained beyond the summer of 1760. A few weeks after Miss Talbot's visit he was laid low by a paralytic stroke, and, attended by Mr. Stafford Crane and "the last of our learned physicians," Dr. William Heberden, died on the fourth of July at Parson's Green, Fulham. Thither to an "old House and neglected Garden," reputed to have been Queen Katharine of Arragon's dower-house (and now vanished), he had moved his country-establishment, with grotto complete, on 30 October, 1754. For all his short expectation of life, the sturdy livery-man preferred to pay £300 over the removal, rather than submit to what he considered an extortionate raising of his rent for the North End house from £25 to £40 *per annum.*

Chapter Two

CIRCLE, CHARACTER, AND OPINIONS

§ 1

Richardson's death caused little stir. There were no unusual happenings to mark his burial in the centre aisle of St. Bride's, Salisbury Court, on 10 July ; and neither public press nor private correspondence took notice of the occurrence. Certain more devoted friends, like Lady Bradshaigh, must have felt a little hurt by this neglect and at any rate expected Edward Young, a man of letters, an admirer and an acquaintance of his, to write a Memoir, for which he had ample materials, or, if he would not do that, at the very least to compose his epitaph. He did neither. Mrs. Carter, to be sure, produced an epitaph— which the curious may read in Mrs. Barbauld's pages— but the family did not use it. So faithful, puzzled, well-meaning Lady Bradshaigh felt urged to express her indignation and, at the same time, supply the deficiency with the following verses :

" On Mr. R———n.

An humble attempt, from a gratful heart.

Waiting for abler hands thy worth to paint,
My longing hand forebore—but now bless'd Saint

32

I must attempt—unequal to the task—
Again rein'd in by diffidence I ask—
Why sleeps the pen of young ! the friend profess'd,
The known abillities, the knowing best
That heart, which few can equal, none excell,
That heart, which lov'd thee and thou lov'd'st so well.
His humbler friends expected, wish'd, and waited,
To hear from thee his character compleated.
Yet why ! can even young, in thought sublime,
Soar above Harlow, Grandison,—What time,
What genious can Illust'rate such a man ?
In morals pure, Religion most Intense,
What more ! A Christian in the noblest sense."

Nothing was done with this effusion either.

The reason for this apparent disfavour is, it may be con-
jectured, twofold : first, seven years had gone by since he
had published any work of importance ; secondly, as
there are good grounds for supposing, certain unamiable
qualities had gained the upper hand in his character and
his closer acquaintances, those who had something to do
in setting the *ton*, had been alienated. Besides, the disfavour is more apparent to us than to contemporaries.
Even royalty was buried in the eighteenth century
amid public indifference, and, however much Richardson
himself had done to stimulate personal emotionalism,
the factitious public counterpart was happily undreamed
of.

Richardson died, then, and was buried, as he had lived,
unostentatiously. For more than fifty years his had been
the life of the Virtuous Tradesman, who, born at a time
of family misfortunes and aspiring to answer a higher call,
had followed a lowly but honourable trade, had prospered

in it, had married his master's daughter, begotten a numerous family to rear in godliness and useful occupation and done what in him lay to leave the world a better place than he found it. Even after the publication and applause of *Pamela* he made no figure in the public eye ; silent and ill at ease in company, he became neither the centre nor a permanent member of any remarkable, well defined set, who might knead him into a legend and transmit that legend in chaplets of anecdotes, as the Johnsonian legend was handed down a few years later.

§ 2

Who his friends were, we do not know. Most likely he had none. On the other hand, he was the man to have many acquaintances. Most of them belong to one or other of three groups : his trade-connexions, with whom one may link his family-connexions, his literary correspondents, and his " female senate."

About his business connexions, who probably furnished his closest intimacies, we know least : for them there were no long, flowery letters, which daughter Patty could copy and file ; they left no Memoirs behind. Foremost among them, leastways in his later years, we may with some propriety reckon the three executors of his will : Andrew Millar, the bookseller, Fielding's publisher, for whom it is reasonable to suppose that he did much printing ; Alington Wilde, his brother-in-law ; and Francis Gosling, of Gosling's Bank, who began life as a bookseller and, becoming Lord Mayor, ended it as Sir Francis. Gosling forms a tie with a friend of earlier days, Charles Rivington, of whom mention has already been made ; for at his death on 22 February, 1742, Rivington appointed Richardson, as one of his executors, guardian to his infant children: and his son John Rivington (who, however, was never a ward of Richardson's) married Francis Gosling's sister.

§ 3

Discounting those shadowy gentlemen or noblemen (who may perhaps be boiled down to one, and he the Duke of Wharton), who, Richardson alleged, befriended him in or before the seventeen-twenties, the earliest of Richardson's literary acquaintanceships was that with Aaron Hill, who very probably introduced him to other men of letters, —members in their turn of yet other circles not disinclined to welcome the author of *Pamela*. Hill, playwright, versifier and pamphleteer, was one of those eccentric philanthropoid individualists who flourished most happily in the eighteenth century. To-day, he is forgotten by all but the historian, and the historian remembers him chiefly as the popularizer of Voltaire on the English stage. But his activities covered a very extensive field : he wrote a long poem on the Duke of Marlborough (which at one time carried the arresting title of *Go to Bed, Tom !* and then the feeble one of *The Fanciad*) ; he paraphrased part of the Sermon on the Mount into heroic couplets; he corresponded with Pope and Garrick ; he tried to introduce viniculture into the marshy environs of Plaistow, and nearly two hundred years ago he advocated the foundation of just such an Academy of Dramatic Art as now flourishes in Gower Street. Richardson and he seem to have come into contact over the printing of one or other of his works, and for nearly fifteen years they carried on an interchange of courteous queries and compliments.

SAMUEL RICHARDSON

Though the fact cannot be proved, it seems likely that it was through Hill that Richardson got to know Colley Cibber and David Mallet as well as the family of Arthur Onslow, the Speaker ; through the Onslows he made the acquaintanceship of Thomas Edwards. The relations between the old " irreclaimable sinner of Seventy-nine," as Lady Bradshaigh called Cibber in a letter of 1751, one of the last and by no means least representative survivors of Restoration days, and the strait-laced burgess of Salisbury Square, are uncertain and somewhat strange. The author of *Shamela*, whether he be Fielding or another, certainly believed that Colley Cibber had written *Pamela* (just as others suspected Hill), and in *Joseph Andrews* Fielding's satire of the same book is closely associated with that of Cibber's *Apology*, also published in 1740. Later, equally singular to say, Cibber, " liking Pamela, was very drawn to see " the first draft of *Clarissa*, which threw him into such violent raptures that he had a vision of Heaven— or so he said. He was consulted about the conduct of that story ; and it seems clear from Lady Bradshaigh's indignant epithets just quoted that *Grandison* was submitted to his judgment before publication also. Something distinctly resembling an affinity between the two on the plane of literary history will be indicated in another place. It may account for the surprising personal sympathy they seem to have felt for one another.

Another unlikely friend of Cibber's who was associated in many ways with Richardson, is Edward Young (1683-1765.) Like Cibber and Hill he was constantly and seriously consulted over the progress of *Clarissa*. His *Night Thoughts* had an international vogue and an after fame in histories of literature very similar to that enjoyed by *Pamela* and *Clarissa* ; and that work, on its first

36

appearance, had in part been printed at Richardson's press. The footing on which the two stood remains none too clear. Richardson appeared to claim a considerable intimacy with Young, which, as we have seen, his friends also supposed. His letters are full of meetings in town, at Barnet and at Welwyn, where Young had the living. Young, on the other hand, insisted that they met but rarely and evidently wished to leave the impression of a distant relationship. But he was old and tired when the claims of an acquaintanceship extinguished by death threatened to become onerous, and it would seem that on the whole Richardson's view of it comes nearer the truth than Young's. For fifteen years, as we know from the surviving documents, they were in close communication ; it was to Richardson that Young wanted to read *The Brothers,* so that he might judge of its effect, and it was in the form of an open letter to him that he published his very striking *Essay on Original Composition* after requiring and receiving what he described as " masterly assistance " in detailed criticism of the whole—criticism, it may be noted, which substantially toned down the radicalism of the first drafts. Moreover, the only authentic portrait of Young known to exist, that at All Souls College, was a present which he made to Richardson, and that, after all, was a somewhat expensive token of regard for a mere distant *confrère* to bestow.

Apart from the one matter of the *Essay on Original Composition* the letters exchanged between Richardson and Young are barren of literary interests. From this point of view perhaps the least disappointing is his correspondence with Thomas Edwards—though, to be sure, the world would be little the poorer if it too had perished. Thomas Edwards (1699-1757), a well-to-do dilettante, living at Terrick between Tring and Prince's Risboro', spent his time studying Spenser, Shakespeare and Milton, girding at the Augustan critics, practising the art of the sonnet (for which he won several converts among Richardson's other acquaintances) and, altogether, unobtrusively clearing the channels of that subterraneous " Romantic " current, whose steady flow throughout the eighteenth century is at last receiving proper attention. Richardson and he found much in common in running down Fielding and deploring the taste that could approve him, as well as in furthering more positively what they called the literature of the " heart." Often pressed by Richardson to winter in his suburban villa, Edwards at last responded to his invitation after the removal to Parson's Green ; he spent the winter of 1755-6 there, and it was unluckily there, too, that he " commenced immortal," as his host phrased it, on 4 January, 1757.

Edwards's poetic gift and his estimation of his friend may be seen in the following poem, first printed in the second edition of *Grandison* :

Sweet moralist ! whose generous labours tend,
With ceaseless diligence, to guide the mind,
In the wild maze of error wandering blind,
To virtue, truth, and honour, glorious end
Of glorious toils ! Vainly would I commend,
In numbers worthy of your sense refin'd,
This last great work, which leaves all praise behind,
And justly stiles you of mankind the friend :

Pleasure with profit artful while you blend,
And now the fancy, now the judgment feed,
With grateful change, with every passion sways ;

Numbers who ne'er to graver lore attend,
Caught by the charm, grow virtuous as they read,
And lives reform'd shall give you genuine praise.

Edwards's most enduring work was that attack on Warburton's methods of criticism which Johnson contemptuously likened to a fly stinging " a stately horse." To Edwards accordingly we may attribute, in some measure at least, the alienation of Richardson from Warburton, whose support at one time he courted. Warburton, the critic and divine, had condescended to *Pamela*, when the author pushed a handsome set under his nose, and had then written a Preface for the first edition of *Clarissa*. He had however taken umbrage at two particulars in the body of that work that seemed to impugn his recently deceased friend Pope : first, the repudiation of the famous epigram that " Every woman is at heart a rake " and, second, the allusion to " the celebrated Bard, who aiming at more than his due is refused the honour he may justly claim," which, Richardson later confessed, *was* directed against Pope. After this Richardson became friendly with the stinging Edwards, whose Sonnet " O Master of the heart " was printed as introductory matter to *Clarissa* at the same time as Warburton's Preface was dropped, and Warburton, accordingly, cut him in a scene which Richardson amusingly describes in a letter to Edwards of 21 April, 1753.

The mention of Warburton and Edwards naturally leads on to a consideration of Richardson's relations with Samuel Johnson, one aspect of which has already been touched upon in describing Richardson's contribution to *The Rambler*. Direct evidence of frequent intercourse is scanty, but what there is suggests a fairly close intimacy.

SAMUEL RICHARDSON

It was Richardson whose help Johnson invoked,—nor invoked it in vain,—when under an arrest for £5 18s. :— and it was to Richardson's practice that the greatest critic of the age almost always would refer as a criterion when he spoke of the novelist's art, pronouncing him " to be the greatest genius that has shed its lustre on this path of literature." Friends of Johnson's at this time were also acquaintances of Richardson's : such as Anna Williams, who had her " Verses to Mr. Richardson on his History of Sir Charles Grandison " (after revision by Johnson) printed in *The Gentleman's Magazine* for January 1754 ; Hogarth, who first met Johnson at Richardson's ; and Giuseppe Baretti, who called him one of the best friends he had in England and who was no doubt laid under contribution for the Italian local colour of *Sir Charles Grandison*.

§ 4

The female set which applauded Richardson and which he gratified with his attentions, while Mrs. Richardson added curtseys " *qui ne finissent point*," was a vague entity consisting of a fairly stable nucleus of ladies always or regularly in London and a number of comet-like individuals who rushed in at lengthy intervals from Cheltenham, Rochester and such places. Its establishment may have been due to Mrs. Delany, whose second husband, Dr. Delany, Richardson got to know over the printing of his *Life of David*, if not of his *Reflections upon Polygamy*. It was a large set. After naming in his Will thirty-two persons to whom mourning-rings of the value of one guinea should be given he adds : " Had I Bequeathed a Ring to each of the Ladies I was honoured by as Correspondents and treuly [sic] Venerate for their Virtues and Amiable Qualities, the list of their names would even in this solemn Act have subjected me to the charge of Ostentation." The constant member for whom, apparently, Richardson cared most was the beautiful Hester Mulso (1727—1801). Richardson paid her the great compliment of using her as the model for Harriet Byron and perhaps for Clarissa Harlowe as well. That this had its drawbacks too emerges from the malicious observation of Mrs. Delany's that " Richardson's *high admiration for her* has made him take her *as a model* for his genteel characters, and that is the reason they *are not* so really polished as he thinks them to be."

Miss Mulso, as Mrs. Chapone, became celebrated as one of the leaders of the Bluestockings ; and though Richardson did not know the veterans of that brigade, Mrs. Vesey, Mrs. Montagu and Mrs. Boscawen, he could pride himself on doing a good deal towards female emancipation, at all events in the republic of letters. He encouraged " his ladies " not only to talk on general questions and so know themselves, as he put it ; he also urged them to write—and more guileless and insipid manuscripts than we know of must have passed through his palsied hands. Miss Mulso, for instance, cast her dissertations on *Filial Obedience and the Matrimonial Creed* into the form of three very lengthy letters to him.

Such encouragement it was, however, not necessary to bestow on the most distinguished of his female friends, Mrs. Carter, who translated Epictetus and impressed Dr. Johnson. They became acquainted through Richardson's purloining her " Ode to Wisdom " for *Clarissa*, having been unable to trace the author : Mrs. Carter protested, received a formal apology and an author's set of the whole novel and later became a visitor at Salisbury Court and North End, though one is left with the impression that she did not much like her host.

Susannah Highmore, the daughter of the painter Joseph Highmore (an acquaintance of Richardson's) and herself possessed of some draughtsmanship, made an amusingly naive picture which is to be found reproduced as frontispiece of this volume. It represents Richardson reading some of his early work on *Grandison* aloud to an audience in that famous grotto of his at North End. Beside the artist, there were present : Miss Mulso, her friend Miss Prescott, her brother Mr. Edward Mulso, who later married the said Miss Prescott, Mr. Mulso *père* and Mr. Duncombe, the author of the *Feminiad or Female Genius*, who ten patient years later married Susannah Highmore herself.

To those already enumerated should be added many more, only a minority of whom of course are known by name ; they fall into two groups : the bluestockings or authors, like Sarah Fielding, Henry's sister (who brought three less gifted sisters with her), Margaret Collier, who collaborated with her in *The Cry* and independently wrote *The Art of Tormenting*, Charlotte Lennox, the author of *The Female Quixote*, Mrs. Sheridan, the brilliant mother of a brilliant son and herself a novelist after Richardson's heart and style ; and, on the other hand, some pleasant enough " young things " who invested him with a honorary paternity and sat listening in dumb amazement, such as Sarah or Selena Wescomb, a fatherless girl whom Richardson " gave away " when she married Mr. Scudamore.

§ 5

Of all Richardson's many feminine acquaintances only one appears to have wrought upon his emotions : that was Lady Bradshaigh. The homely-looking wife of a good-natured Lancashire baronet, Sir Roger Bradshaigh, of Haigh, she became passionately concerned about the fate of Clarissa Harlowe, as it was being serially unfolded. Pretending to be a Mrs. Belfour of Warrington, she emboldened herself to write, in a not uncommon confusion of thought between prophecy and destiny, to the " Editor " of Clarissa's papers, beseeching him to spare her life and to have poetic justice meted out to her in the end. Though Richardson took no notice of her representations in so far as his narrative was concerned, he followed up her letter in his private capacity and, the correspondence once started, it continued even after Clarissa was miserably dead, buried and avenged. It fills the equivalent of a Folio volume at South Kensington and, clearly, at one time there was more of it. Soon, " Mrs. Belfour " demanded to set eyes on the being who could so powerfully excite her. Richardson answered not without coquetry, describing himself and stating when and where he would be visible. The lady accordingly saw him in February, 1750 and formally met him during the next month, when, of course, her own disguise had to be discarded.

The personal introduction involved no slackening in the correspondence, since Lady Bradshaigh spent little time in London. To her above all others he attributed the stimulus which drove him to the composition of *Sir Charles Grandison*, and she was kept as much *au courant* with its progress as his somewhat secretive habits would permit.

43

After its completion, as has been noted in the first chapter, she urged him to undertake yet another novel of similar magnitude, and, this proving vain, to other enterprises which, while sparing his health, should still keep his name before the public. Letters on these and other topics of common interest continued until the latter half of 1760.

Lady Bradshaigh seems to have been a blunt, jolly sort of woman, very little of a bluestocking ; but, proud as she was—and a little frightened—of knowing an author and possessing his portrait, there is no evidence that she cared for him as a person at all. In 1757 Richardson complains, with mixed pathos and peevishness, that though Lady Bradshaigh had been in London on a seven months' visit, she has only called on him once in all that time and then stayed half-an-hour or less :—from which we may conclude also that the author of *Grandison* was getting somewhat tiresome in personal intercourse. His feelings for her, on the other hand, seem to have gone—a little— but only a little—beyond that sentimental or playful effusiveness he always had at command for others. On one occasion he writes :

" Every Saturday that I go thro' St. James's Park . . . how do I mark the Places that my Eye puts down for this, and for that Spot, where I have been so happy as to see a certain beloved Correspondent ! Did I tell you, Madam, that I make Broad-street, now and then, tho' out of my Way, *in* my Way, on purpose to see a certain House, which at a certain time I delighted to approach ? "

But the most conclusive evidence of his feeling for her is to be found in an endorsement of one of her surviving letters. As a practical joke, Richardson had apparently threatened to kill off the heroine of *Sir Charles Grandison* just as he had killed off Clarissa, whereupon Lady Bradshaigh conceived the same distress as had made her disregard decorum five years earlier. Richardson was smitten with remorse at his callous frivolity and, with shaking hand, scrawled over the back of her letter what looks like :

" last Agonies, occasioned by a private and unexpected Stab given to a beloved Friend, whom I looked upon as the sweet Companion of my retired Hours ; my Guide, my Instructress ; my Repose in Weariness : my Joy in Trouble ; my guide, my Instructor. I awaked in T . . . ."

§ 6

This would be the appropriate place at which to quote that self-description just mentioned, which excellently supplements the Frontispiece to this book :

" Short ; rather plump than emaciated, notwithstanding his complaints : about five foot five inches : fair wig ; lightish cloth coat, all black besides : one hand generally in his bosom, the other a cane in it, which he leans upon under the skirts of his coat usually, that it may imperceptibly serve him as a support, when attacked by sudden tremors or startings, and dizziness, which too frequently attack him, but, thank God, not so often as formerly : looking directly foreright, as passers-by would imagine, but observing all that stirs on either hand of him without moving his short neck ; hardly ever turning back : of a light-brown complexion ; teeth not yet failing

45

him ; smoothish faced, and ruddy cheeked : at sometimes looking to be about sixty-five, at other times much younger : a regular even pace, stealing away ground, rather than seeming to rid it : a grey eye, too often over-clouded by mistinesses from the head : by chance lively ; very lively it will be, if he have hope of seeing a lady whom he loves and honours : his eye always on the ladies ; if they have very large hoops, he looks down and supercilious, and as if he would be thought wise, but perhaps the sillier for that : as he approaches a lady, his eye is never fixed first upon her face, but upon her feet, and thence he raises it up, pretty quickly for a dull eye ; and one would think (if we thought him at all worthy of observation) that from her air and (the last beheld) her face, he sets her down in his mind as *so* or *so*, and then passes on to the next object he meets ; only then looking back, if he greatly likes or dis-likes, as if he would see if the lady appear to be all of a piece, in the one light or in the other."

§ 7

The character which Richardson revealed in intercourse with his different acquaintances is not very pronounced, or always pleasing. The groundwork of it, however, was solid and honest enough. Richardson genuinely cultivated his friends, honoured their " correspondencies " by treating them like dispatches from foreign courts, to be annotated, glossed, filed and docketed ; he did willingly the countless little offices expected of a friend in town, acting as bank, parcels-office, mail-order store and news-paper—receiving from time to time pleasant requital of his services in game, venison or a cask of cider. Of his business methods we know little, but if his dealings with one Eusebius Silvester, a Warwick attorney who turned out a swindler, afford any clue to others, he was as honourable, far-sighted and open as he was shrewd and practical. He took a genuine and sustained interest in furthering what he conceived as the interests of the young and inexperienced, though his natural " sheepishness " made the outward manifestations of such interest look stiff and often savour of condescension.

All these qualities would, given similar circumstances, have come to the front if Richardson had remained until his death nothing more than the superior printer he had been up to his fifty-first year. What brought out the worst in him was authorship. Nor is that altogether surprising to anyone who bears in mind the phenomenal success of his latter-day labours, the international fame they brought him and the fact that he was prized and lauded for precisely those qualities that lay nearest his own heart, his ethical soundness, his appeal to the emotions and his success in building up what seemed a perfectly new literature on this dual basis. Moreover, for twenty years he was inundated with flatteries from literary pundits like Warburton and Johnson or the anonymous correspondent who wrote only a few months after the publication of *Pamela* : " Tho' I am not Superstitious, I should regard a bit of Paper from your Hands, in the same manner as Bigots do Amulets and Relics of Saints."

The worst in Richardson, though it took several forms, may be summed up in one word, Vanity. " That fellow Richardson," Mrs. Piozzi makes Johnson say, " . . . could not be contented to sail quietly down the stream of reputation without longing to taste the froth from every stroke of the oar." Of this itch of his Boswell's hackneyed illustration is also the most splendid :

" One day . . . a gentleman who had just returned from Paris, willing to please Mr. Richardson, mentioned to him a very flattering circumstance,—that he had seen his *Clarissa* lying on the King's brother's table. Richardson observing that part of the company were engaged in talking to each other, affected then not to attend to it. But by and by, when . . . he thought that the flattery might be fully heard, he addressed himself to the gentleman, ' I think, Sir, you were saying something about,—' pausing in a high flutter of expectation. The gentleman . . . with an exquisitely sly air of indifference answered, ' A mere trifle, Sir, not worth repeating.' "

A cynical investigator might even suspect him of deliberately manufacturing some of the froth of which Dr. Johnson speaks or, at any rate, credit him with an expertness in " publicity," which would cause surprise as occurring in so far distant and pre-Yankee an age, if one did not recollect the amazing career, a few years before, of De Foe, the first of journalists.

The story of Dr. Slocock recommending *Pamela* from the pulpit is sufficiently famous ; less well known are some obscure negotiations between the preacher and the novelist which followed and in which the latter, animated by the emotion defined as " a lively sense of favours to come," took upon himself to buy up one half of a bad debt owing to the former. This, of course, casts no aspersions on Dr. Slocock's enthusiasm for *Pamela*, but it may render Richardson's charity a little suspect, as does his request for a critical verdict which accompanied his gift of the *Edition de luxe* of *Pamela* to Warburton. There is, too, a faint savour of sharp practice about the act of a man who inserts in a paper to which he is printer a puff of a book he himself has written, as Richardson did when a paragraph in *The Weekly Miscellany* for 17 January, 1741 praised the *Familiar Letters* before their publication and gave some excerpts from them. The same thing may be felt and said about an ostensibly non-partisan or even hostile pamphlet, which by the imbecility of its animadversions, really acts, as it was intended to, as veiled advocacy and a stimulant to more wide-spread discussion :—and as such even a fairly candid mind might well look upon *Remarks on Clarissa* and may be also the *Candid Examination of the History of Sir Charles Grandison.*

Perhaps, since they cannot be substantiated, it is unjust to lay stress on the suspicions which transactions like these arouse, however insistent they may be. Certainly taste alone, not the ethical sense, is rendered uneasy by the puffing Letters prefixed to *Pamela* which Fielding derided, while the answer to Haller's criticism of *Clarissa* in *The Gentleman's Magazine* for August 1749, even if written by Richardson himself (as it looks like being) and indirectly profitable to him, is purely unexceptionable. Whatever share he may have had in engineering them, Richardson was certainly lucky in the various oblique ways by which interest in his works was aroused !

An obvious form for vanity such as his to take is jealousy, and jealousy Richardson evinced not merely as a sailor upon the stream of reputation, but also in that peculiarly offensive suspiciousness of ingratitude which poisons the personal relations of many elderly people, whatever their rank and occupation of life. Something of this sort underlay a coolness between Mrs. Delany and Richardson, which subsisted for several months at least. In his ultra-paternal, patronizing manner—" Condescension becomes ye Character of ye Parent," he avowed on another occasion,

—he had been pleased to have Mrs. Delany's god-daughter stay with him and the young lady, lacking as yet the example of Mr. Collins, had been perhaps a little remiss in acknowledging the favour conferred on her : " I find," her godmother writes to Mrs. Dewes on 5 November, 1754, " our poor Sally had disobliged Mr. Richardson by not writing to his wife and children " and adds the significant exclamation " that *fiend jealousy.*" Richardson evidently did not leave it at passive " disobligation " either. On the 16 January, 1756, fourteen months later, Mrs. Delany writes, again to Mrs. Dewes : " I have seen Mr. Richardson but once, and his family once : they have not behaved kindly to Sally, particularly Mr. Richardson." Obligation, according to a well-known frame of mind, can be paid for, but it is disgraceful of the vendor not to throw infinite good will into the bargain !

§ 8

Richardson's professional jealousy is notorious. It showed itself in a steady belittlement of all contemporaries catering for the same public as himself. The words " novels " and " romances "—except when in (mistaken) commendation they might be applied to his own productions—were, to him, terms of abuse ; their authors, " the Behn's, the Manley's and the Heywood's " just " a set of Wretches." Though he printed for Smollett, his only reference to his works of fiction is to " that Part of a bad Book [clearly *Peregrine Pickle*] which contains the very bad story of a wicked woman [the inset-story of Lady Vane] " which early in 1751 he sends to Mrs. Chapone senior for her son with the hint : " I could be glad to see it animadverted upon by so admirable a Pen." Sterne and Rousseau, two rivals appearing on the scene when his own career was almost run, immediately came under his lash : of the former he said, more charitably and justly than he intended : " One extenuating circumstance attends his works, that they are too gross to be inflaming."

Henry Fielding, however, he felt with true divination to be his greatest competitor and it is against him that he and sycophantic friends of his rage most furiously. To be sure, Fielding started the broil, if not with *Shamela*, then with *Joseph Andrews* ; and for these " lewd and ungenerous ingraftments " the author of *Pamela* never forgave him, though Fielding made at least two overtures to reconciliation, showing a respectful interest in the sufferings of Clarissa Harlowe during the months in which the uncertainty of her fate was perturbing the public and openly declaring with apparent approval in his *Covent-Garden Journal* : " *Pleasantry* (as the ingenious Author of Clarissa says of a Story) *should be made only the Vehicle of Instruction*." The fundamental trouble was that Fielding had wider conceptions of Pleasantry and Instruction than Richardson, his tolerance could be amused where Richardson must rail or weep ; he held the doubtful or at any rate dangerous view that a man may speak Truth with a smiling face and he embodied this maxim in his novels, which, combining Humour and Truth, where Richardson could only yoke Truth with a sometimes dubious Pathos, vexatiously appealed to the frivolous as well as the serious-minded. Now " a jest at vice by virtue's called a crime." So Richardson, though he professed not to have sullied his mind by reading them, did all that lay within his power to decry *Joseph Andrews*, *Tom Jones* and *Amelia*. He wrote round to his friends for denunciatory criticisms and, if these were not sufficiently damning, expostulated. He declared that Fielding wrote principally to fill his pockets, whereas Avarice had never been a motive with *him*. He called Tom Jones and Sophia Western names. He crowed with joy when *Amelia* inexplicably failed and its author left the arena :

" Mr. Fielding," he wrote to Edwards, " has met with the disapprobation you foresaw he would meet with, of his Amelia. He is, in every paper he publishes under the title of the Common Garden, contributing to his own over throw. He has been overmatched in his own way by people whom he had despised, and when he thought he had vogue enough, from the success his spurious brat Tom Jones so unaccountably met with, to write down ; but who have turned his own artillery against him, and beat him out of the field, and made him even poorly in his Court of Criticism, give up his Amelia, and promise to write no more on the like subjects."

He inserted marginal notes in the files of his correspondence to make it quite clear that depreciatory epithets were meant for Fielding ; and (no doubt) he purred as loudly as he had crowed when Anna Williams published (during Fielding's life-time too) those verses of hers in *The Gentleman's Magazine*, in which she confidently prophesied :

" In distant times, when *Jones* and *Booth* are lost, Britannia her *Clarissa's* name shall boast,"

and when Mr. Edwards vented one of his greatest ineptitudes to the effect that " the fellow "—whose posthumous *Voyage to Lisbon* had just appeared—" had no heart.

And so—his knell is knoll'd." It is amusing to find that Richardson founded his dislike of Fielding in part on what to-day seems one of his grandest qualities, exclaiming in his last letter to Aaron Hill that " he is a very indelicate, a very impetuous, an *unyielding-spirited Man.*"

§ 9

We come now to one of the few really important problems in connection with Richardson's biography where the evidential material proves insufficient. How much, namely, did he really know about the literature which he condemned, how much did he know of literature in general ? His own statements in reply to questions like these cannot be accepted without reserve. He would, for instance, indignantly disavow all knowledge of Fielding's writings, but if his correspondents were too sparing in their horror and denunciations he found himself well able to draw their attention to what they had overlooked. Again, he complained that after reaching man's estate he had little time for reading and that, in fact, he read little, having " a Head so little able to bear it." " What stores of knowledge do I lose, by my incapacity of reading," he groans to Miss Highmore. But three reservations—which between them may admit almost anything—must be made to the generalization he would have liked accepted, that he had no commerce with literature at all : first, that he read much in his youth ; second, in Lady Bradshaigh's words, that he had " converse with those who read, and on whose judgment he could depend : " and third, the concessive part of his own statement to Hill, that he read very little *except* in the course of business, What may he not have read in that way ? May not he, for instance, have printed Fielding's novels for Andrew Millar and read them in proof ?

Even Dr. Poetzsche's incomplete monograph on Richardson's reading makes it abundantly clear that whatever his sources of information, Richardson commanded a store of quotable tags from, and allusions to, English writers, which would be considered very respectable to-day. It must not be assumed, all the same, that this store implies any thorough knowledge : Richardson, one imagines after studying his works, treated English literature rather as all but the foremost classics of the time treated Latin and Greek literature, as a convenient repository of chapter-heads and paragraph conclusions. His own selection may have been, probably was, derived from a commonplace-book which he seems to have compiled as a young man and on which he drew copiously for *Pamela, Part II ;* some of it he found ready-made for him by the periodical essayists so popular in his day. *The Spectator*, he tells us, was the joy of his prentice days, though in maturer years he came to prefer *The Rambler*. He owned interleaved copies of *The Plain Dealer* and *The Prompter* (the latter written by Aaron Hill alone, the former by him in collaboration with William Bond). These and their like, while aggravating his moralistic bias, would at the same time furnish him out with a good deal of quotable matter, but on one point, as it is important to realize in the twentieth century, they would scarcely enlighten him, even at second-hand, namely on the trend of current literature in general. The book-review was as unknown in his day as the serial publication of larger pieces of literature in magazines or reviews—both innovations popularized in this country by Smollett after Richardson's writing days were over. On the other hand, there is some slight evidence that, in his youth at all events, Richardson was a play-goer : his conception of high and highish society may well have derived from the tarnished reflection of Restoration manners exhibited in the theatres of Queen Anne and George I. He possessed sufficient knowledge of English History to pass " judicious remarks on the Plan " of Smollett's work. With everyone else at that time, he had what seems to us a morbid appetite for sermons and works like *Pluralities Indefensible* " by a good and honest Clergyman." To please Edwards he rubbed up such knowledge of Spenser, Shakespeare and Milton's poetry as he had acquired (Milton's prose he could not abide), and he had the sagacity to opine that Theobald would make a better editor of Shakespeare than Pope. He read, we know, the revised version of *The Dunciad* and Whitehead's *Essay on Ridicule.* He preferred *Cooper's Hill* to *Windsor Forest;* in his old age he admired the poetry of Gray, though he equally thought that Mr. Mason had *a fine Genius.* And there are one or two other works of belles lettres with which some familiarity may reasonably be inferred ; among them it is worth noting the Letters of Mme. de Sévigné and of Ninon de l'Enclos. His specific relations with earlier fiction must receive attention in another chapter.

The attitude which Richardson took up to literature and, we may infer, to art in general was closely utilitarian : he valued the products of the imagination in proportion as they conveyed a rule of behaviour, as they warned and exhorted and confirmed in good living. His exemplar, Clarissa, we are told, " used to lament that certain writers of the first class, who were capable of exalting virtue, and of putting vice out of countenance, too generally employed themselves in works of *imagination only,* upon subjects *merely speculative, disinteresting, and unedifying,* from which no useful moral or example could be drawn . . . she often pitied the celebrated Dr. Swift for so employing his admirable pen, that a pure eye was afraid of looking into his works, and a pure ear from hearing anything quoted from them." So her creator confined his admiration of Pope, whom the fashion of the age bade him admire in some form or other, to his Versification and that very vague thing, his Genius,—" But forgive me, Sir, to say, I am scandaliz'd for human Nature, and such Talents, sunk so low." In writing to Edwards he wisely sticks most of the time to rhetorical generalities when touching on the great names of literature. " O that Spenser, Milton, Shakespeare, may be handed down in their own unborrowed Lights to latest Times ! " he exclaims, and, of his correspondent's favourite Spenser, in particular, " were but his language better understood, he must be admired by every one who has a heart."

§ 10

Similarly unfruitful was the commerce of his mind with questions of morals and statecraft. He neither questioned the usual political and ethical code of the middle classes nor departed from it, unless it be perhaps in the very elementary humanitarianism which he shared with Sir Charles Grandison, the practical opponent of docking horses' tails. If ever he was, as Negus hinted, a " high-flyer," he emancipated himself so far from the Toryism of his young manhood as to identify Whig with loyalty, and Tory with sedition. His distrust of Carteret, how-ever, leads one to suppose that, in his opinion, the hey-day of the Whigs passed with the fall of Sir Robert Walpole ; but in any case, he soon " laid aside so contemptible a subject as politics," while reserving himself the right to judge, with equal impartiality, Hume and Bolingbroke as very mischievous writers.   In foreign affairs, he upheld the policy of William III by urging a close alliance between England and the United Provinces, which he would have liked to see strengthened by the inclusion of the present Belgium and parts of Northern France, all under the sway of a " Prince of the Nassau House." The realm of Louis XV *per contra* he wished to see split into three distinct Kingdoms at least and he seems to question the sagacity of the Almighty in bestowing so fruitful a soil, so propitious a climate and so commanding a position on nothing more than a " Nation of mischievous Monkeys."   In fighting them Frederick of Prussia was upholding the whole Protestant interest, as Dutch William of glorious memory had done.   Otherwise his writings yield no dicta on domestic or international politics : the campaigns of Charles XII, which showed Fielding the affinities between glory and crime, the expedition to Cartagena which Smollett described, the march of " a certain Adventurer " on Derby, in which Johnson may have taken part, left him equally unmoved ; he betrayed no interest in the attempts made in his life-time to make London civilized by Acts of Parliament and an efficient police-force, none in the Bangorian controversy, or in the ministries of Wesley and Whitefield or in the removal of the walls of his own city which had survived from the Roman occupation.   Nor did he find anything to say about the personalities of those concerned in these events— unless they happened also to be novelists enjoying some incomprehensible popularity as well !   He agreed with Fielding, all the same, in advocating far-reaching prison-reform ; and he had heard enough of Stephen Hales's experiments to declare him, characteristically, " one of the . . . usefullest genius, that ever graced a court, or a nation." What is most surprising in this list of almost unvaried negatives is the apathy towards religious matters, then so closely allied to his pet subject of morals. On one occasion he remarked with delightful ingenuousness that he shunned probing into the doctrine of the Trinity for fear of the doubts he might raise in himself ! On no account would he risk losing his complacency.

Chapter Three

THE THREE NOVELS AND THEIR PURPOSE

§ 1

According to a laudable custom of the time, the title-page of Richardson's first novel sets forth in full its nature and purpose :[1]

Pamela : or, Virtue Rewarded. In a Series of Familiar Letters from a Beautiful Young Damsel, to her Parents. Now first published in order to cultivate the Principles of Virtue and Religion in the Minds of the Youth of Both Sexes. A Narrative which has its Foundation in Truth and Nature ; and at the same time that it agreeably entertains, by a Variety of curious and affecting Incidents, is intirely divested of all those Images, which, in too many Pieces calculated for Amusement only, tend to inflame the Minds they should instruct.

The process involving the Reward of Virtue may be summarized as follows :

At the age of fifteen, Pamela Andrews, the daughter of honest parents who have come down in the world, loses by death her kind patroness, in whose domestic service she has acquired many mental and moral accomplishments. As, in addition, she possesses good looks and good manners,

[1] No attempt is made exactly to reproduce the typography of this and other title-pages.

59

she attracts the attention of the lady's son and heir, Mr. B——, who forthwith desires to lie with her. The bulk of the book is taken up with a description of the stout resistance which her pious chastity puts up against the assaults and stratagems aimed against it. Mr. B—— proceeds to separate Pamela from her friends, Mrs. Jervis, the housekeeper, and Mr. Longman, the steward, by dispatching her from his Bedfordshire house to B——Hall in Lincolnshire, over which presides his housekeeper Mrs. Jewkes, a tyrant with the proclivities of a bawd. There he keeps her virtually a prisoner, in such wretchedness and fear that, despite the ineffectual friendship of Mr. Williams, the chaplain, she is nearly driven to suicide. Then, when he imagines her spirit must be broken, he hastens to Lincolnshire himself. He successively offers her handsome terms to become his *maîtresse en titre*, attempts to ravish her and plans a mock wedding, all in order to gain his point. Ultimately, however, her steadfast insistence on her virtue, as well as her undeniable affection for him, which, try as she may, she cannot stifle, induce him to drop his dishonourable designs. He bestows upon her the status of lawful wife, a "reward which often, even in this life, a protecting Providence bestows on goodness," and also brings hostile public opinion (led by his termagant sister Lady Davers) over to the side of virtue when introduced to her good-natured and humble piety.

§ 2

It has already been noted that, at the time when he conceived *Pamela*, Richardson had in mind a true story of similar events, which had been told him fifteen years before and which he had urged various friends to cast into literary form. What was this story? There is no conclusive answer to the question. Since from the beginnings of society men have failed to seduce servant-girls and then married them, it is perhaps hardly necessary to point to any one specific "source." Moreover, there were plenty of literary prototypes available. On the other hand, public opinion at the time of *Pamela's* publication did not hesitate to make identifications between the imaginary and real characters, though it was not unanimous in its ascriptions. One of the most popular candidates for Pamela's part was Hannah Sturges, whom her employer, Sir Arthur Hesilrige, married in 1725 and who died in 1765; and her claim is preserved to this day in the imposing pages of Burke. The lady's story is set forth in a rare octavo book of sixty-seven pages, which the British Museum authorities assign tentatively to the year 1775, though its references to her as still living suggest a date at least ten years earlier.

These *Memoirs of the Life of Lady H——, the Celebrated Pamela* tell us that she was the daughter of an occasional assistant-driver of the Northampton stage coach. At the age of fifteen, in the capacity of scullery-maid, she entered the service of Lady H——, where she "underwent a kind of Purgatory, from the Attempts of some of her Fellow-Servants to kiss her." Just after her sixteenth birthday her lady's son, Sir A. H——, Bart., came down from the University. As she "had Beauties sufficient to attract the Attention of her Master," the cook put it into her head that it lay in her power to become Lady H——. Indeed, Sir A. H—— waylaid her one day on her way to see her parents and, on her father surprising them, declared his love and married her forthwith,

—" which put the old Lady, Sir A——'s Mother, into the utmost Rage and Consternation." The dowager Lady H—— behaved very unpleasantly to her daughter-in-law and tried her best to make her son either repudiate the marriage or effect a separation, by suggesting to him that his wife was no virgin when he married her, but an artful, cunning slut. She was sent away into private lodgings and temptations to an evil life put before her, but she resisted them all and, on giving birth to a son and heir, was publicly acknowledged by her husband and taken into society. Her father was made steward of an estate in the North, and Lady H—— continued a model of female virtue, " an Honour to the present Age."

The story clearly differs in certain notable particulars from Richardson's, chiefly in the part played by the "hero's" mother and the length and nature of the heroine's trials, the version in *Pamela* providing for more pathos than the *Memoirs*. The date of the occurrences and the age of the heroine give some colour to the identification, however—though, to be sure, the author of the *Memoirs*, who does not write as if possessed of much first-hand knowledge, may well have taken a few of the " facts " contained in them from the novelist's " fiction " or similar sources, such as the gossip of Richardson's *entourage*. When asked point-blank whether the story of Pamela was based on Lady Hesilrige's, Richardson answered : " Miss Howe [in *Clarissa*] as well as Pamela was intirely the Creature of my Fancy,"—which amounts to a highly suspicious evasion of the issue.

§ 3

Exactly as if *Pamela* had been published in this year of grace, the discussion which it provoked centred on two particular aspects : the personal, which has just been dealt with, and the moral. The latter is of infinitely greater moment, since it was in the first place as a moralist that the author both privately and publicly wished to be judged. The unheeding many, of course, took all its teaching at face value, but a few were found intent on probing beneath the surface. Richardson had announced that he proposed to "cultivate the Principles of Virtue and Religion," and in this aim he signally failed, in the opinion not only of those heretics who dared to differ from him on fundamentals, but also of certain enthusiasts for the same sort of morality as himself.

The criticism of the latter was set forth with equal vigour and justice in a booklet which ran through two editions in the year after the publication of *Pamela*, 1741, and was entitled *The Virgin in Eden ; or, the State of Innocency*. Its author was Charles Povey, a religious mystic and, at the same time, the perfecter of fire-insurance. Povey peremptorily refused all truck with the Devil, arguing that the very Reward of such temptingly assailed Virtue would render the public more complaisant to the wiles of the tempter, which, in prudence, it should avoid rather than await in the assurance of triumph. To his way of thinking, Pamela really lacked the virtue of modesty for which she was extolled in confidently continuing her exposure to the stratagems of Mr. B—— :

"That Maid," he sternly maintained, "who holds a Parley with a vicious Man a second time, and suffers herself to be immodestly embrac'd, I censure her Chastity : She may be compar'd to one of the fair Apples of *Sodom*, beautiful for the Eye to behold, but Stains and Rottenness, within."

Moreover, even if the ethical end be granted, it would not justify all the means. Povey singles out for condemnation three incidents : firstly, a scene in the summer-house of his Bedfordshire estate, when Mr. B——, though suitably rebuked for it, put his arm about Pamela and kissed her " two or three times, with frightful eagerness," afterwards pressing gold into her hand to make amends for the fright he put her in ; then the sequel a fortnight or so later when, in Mrs. Jervis's room, he offered to take her on his knee, by force kissed her neck and lips and then put his hand in her bosom ; thirdly, the notorious incident which Pamela most circumstantially relates in her Journal, how, with wicked Mrs. Jewkes's connivance, Mr. B——, pretending to be the tipsy maid Nan, climbed into the bed which Pamela and Mrs. Jewkes shared and, while the old house-keeper held her down, endeavoured to perpetrate upon her a rape which only a dead faint prevented. " These Scenes," Povey exclaims,

" are Paradoxes to me, to be printed and called *Virtue rewarded*. Good God ! Can amorous Embraces deline-ated in these Images, tend to inculcate Religion in the Minds of Youth, when the Blood is hot, and runs quick in every Vein ? Are these Lights to direct the Soul to a crucify'd Jesus ? Are they Pictures to extinguish Vice, and restrain the Wickedness of the Times ? Will such Representations divert Men of Pleasure from looking on beautiful Women ? Can immodest Intrigues divert lewd Thoughts, and bring off with Honour vicious Minds ? Can a Man, expressing licentious Speeches in Converse with a Maid not yet deflower'd, reform the Age, or inspire Ideas in the Mind worthy of Example ? "

The other general judgment on the teaching of *Pamela*— the kind that questions the value of the self-righteous chastity for which the heroine stands and believes the mental processes attributed to her to be outside nature— has received more attention, because Fielding's first novel was written to embody it. But it found other expressions than *Joseph Andrews*. The anonymous author, for instance, of the *Lettre sur Pamela* (1742), at one with Povey in doubting the complete purity of the heroine and in disparaging the pretexts under which she continues to expose herself to persecution by Mr. B——, clearly indicates with his gentle irony that much too much ado is made about nothing. A similar line is carried much farther by the author of the English *Anti-Pamela : or, Feign'd Innocence detected* (1741), which describes without any indignation the wanton, blackmailing career of Syrena Tricksy, a young person who in disposition and manner has superficially a good deal of resemblance to Pamela Andrews.

But the most searching and destructive criticism of *Pamela* was offered by the pseudonymous author of *Shamela*, published on 4 April, 1741 : he not only, by implication, ridicules the solemnity with which Richardson invested erotic peccadilloes, but also directly impugns his psychological groundwork. This is shown by the title-page, which is worth quoting in full for a variety of reasons :

An Apology for the Life of Mrs. Shamela Andrews. In which, the many notorious Falshoods and Misrepresentations of a Book called Pamela, Are exposed and refuted ; and all the matchless Arts of that young Politician set in a true and just Light. Together with A full Account of all that passed between her and Parson Arthur Williams ; whose Character is represented in a manner something different from that which he bears in Pamela. The whole

SAMUEL RICHARDSON

being exact Copies of authentick Papers delivered to the Editor. Necessary to be had in all Families. By Mr. Conny Keyber, London : *Printed for A. Dodd, at the* Peacock, *without* Temple-Bar. M.DCC.XLI.

The body of this booklet of seventy-one pages begins with a letter from one Parson Tickletext in London to the rural Parson Oliver, recommending *Pamela* to him in such a way that the inflammatory nature of the book is indirectly revealed at once. Upon ' this letter follows the Reverend Mr. Oliver's reply, in which, after touching on the lascivious images and immoral tendencies of *Pamela*, he roundly declares that the readers of that publication have been imposed on. He himself lives near Squire Booby's (as he expands the surname B———) and knows the real facts about his courtship of his wife, whose real name was not Pamela, but Shamela, and who was the daughter of an orange-seller, Henrietta Maria Honora Andrews. To substantiate his general thesis, he encloses the genuine correspondence that passed between Shamela and Henrietta Maria Honora. From this it appears that Shamela, who had already had a child by Parson Williams, a mighty lecher before the Lord, discovering her employer's lust for her, decided to stand out for a handsome settlement before conceding him any favours. Following the instructions of her highly experienced mother, she preserved herself from Mr. Booby's supreme assault (carried out, but with slightly different result, as reported in *Pamela*) and soon perceived that, with the squire's boundless infatuation for her, she might barter her " vartue " for even more than good cash value. " I thought once," she wrote with true Augustan polish, " of making a little Fortune out of my Person. I now intend to make a

66

great one out of my Virtue." So Squire Booby married her according to plan, without, however, putting a stop to her more delightful connection with Mr. Williams. A post-script to Parson Tickletext's acknowledgement of Parson Oliver's communication states that Mr. Booby has discovered the intrigue and has instituted an action against Mr. Williams in the spiritual courts.

Even this brief outline should show with what extreme cleverness the anonymous author preserved intact the main outlines of the tale told in *Pamela*, while substituting motives and inserting minor incidents much more nearly in accordance with the ways of human nature. Mr. B——— is kept the complete young fool who makes possible the cardinal situation of *Pamela* : only his folly is more thoroughly illuminated ; and not much coarsening of the blended artfulness and artlessness of " that young Politician " is required for turning Pamela into Shamela. How Richardson must have winced when confronted with so unfair and yet so close a parody of his Pamela's " reactions " when she realizes that her cully has followed her from Bedfordshire to Lincolnshire :

" I immediately," she reports to her dear Mamma, " run up into my Room, and stript, and washed, and drest my self as well as I could, and put on my prettiest round-ear'd Cap, and pulled down my Stays, to shew as much as I could of my Bosom, (for Parson *Williams* says, that is the most beautiful part of a Woman) and then I practised over all my Airs before the Glass, and then I sat down and read a Chapter in The Whole Duty of Man."

Who was the author of this brilliant squib ? The only name that has ever been given is that of Fielding,

SAMUEL RICHARDSON

whom Richardson, smarting with the venom and accurate aim of the shafts, confidently designated as his tormentor. Like the author of *Shamela*, indeed, Fielding preferred the obsolescent locutions " hath " and " doth " for " has " and " does," expanded B—— into Booby, amalgamated the satire of Colley Cibber's *Apology for his Life* and allusions to Conyers Middleton's *Life of Cicero* with a parody of *Pamela* ; Fielding, too, actually had a parson-friend, whose sagacity he greatly admired, called Oliver ; and in advertising his *Miscellanies* in 1742, he promised an account of " Jonathan Wyld, Esq ; in which not only his Character, but that of divers other great Personages of his Time, will be set in a just and true Light,"—with which announcement it is instructive to compare the title-page of *Shamela* quoted a page or two back. It seems unlikely that two men with such similar outlook and powers of description should have been living at the same time, and even more so that one of them should never (as would seem) have ventured beyond an anony-mous brochure. So we may safely leave *Shamela* at Fielding's door.

§ 4

Part II of *Pamela*, *Pamela in her Exalted Condition* as it was called after some dallying with the idea of *Pamela in Genteel Life*, is by far the worst thing that Richardson ever wrote, possessing no interest except of a narrowly technical kind to be considered later. After all, the placing of storm-tossed Pamela into a state of relatively stable bliss and the reclamation of Mr. B—— were the object of the First Part, and any sequel which did not stultify the original starts with that almost intolerable handicap. Accordingly, hardly anything happens in the Second Part of *Pamela*, except that Pamela adds parturition and (after a fight with her husband over it) suckling, to the domestic duties which her late mistress had imparted to her. The letters which she writes and receives (there are a hundred and three of them) deal with her wise provision for relatives and other dependents, together with their edifying gratitude in return therefor, the past history of certain correspondents and their friends, Pamela's *ex cathedra* pronouncements upon infantile nutrition, education, public diversions and the like ; no really fresh complications in the realm of matter or of mind arise for discussion, let alone solution, except (if one may call them so) Pamela's distresses at Mr. B——'s crack-brained theory and supposed practice of " polygamy," which it is difficult to understand how even anyone so completely limited as Pamela could take seriously. The kind of thing which fills the two volumes is indicated by the summary given of Letter XX :

" *Mrs. B—— to Lady Davers.*—Sends her the copy of her answer to Miss Darnford, in which she gives ' Mr. ' B——'s reasons why every member of parliament should ' attend the business of it. Presses Miss Darnford to ' winter with them in London. Rallies Sir Simon for ' flinging a book at Miss Darnford's head, and for what ' he calls his innocent double entendres ; and expresses ' how much she is delighted with the account Miss Darn- ' ford gives her of Mrs. Jewkes's penitence.' Then gives her ladyship the copy of her answer to Mrs. Jewkes's letter. ' Rejoicing in her conversion ; encouraging her to ' perseverance ; arming her against despondency, and ' warning her against returning to her former evil ways.' Gives her ladyship an affecting instance of contented poverty and resignation. Her serious reflections upon the unsatisfactory nature of even the highest enjoyments. Is delighted with her ladyship's approbation of her conduct to Miss Goodwin. Generously endeavours to extenuate her [Miss Goodwin's] mamma's fall, and to exalt her merit for her remarkable penitence."

Richardson availed himself of the opportunity which the endless discussions of conduct in *Pamela II* afforded to answer one very common but hitherto unnoticed charge directed against the " moral " of the original *Pamela* : that it would encourage young gentlemen to marry their mothers' maids. With a lack of tact which must be forgiven him in recognition of his hardihood, one of Pamela's guests, Sir Jacob Swynford, brings the very topic on to the carpet. Pamela's peculiar casuistry cannot be better illustrated than by her contribution to this argument. In some countries, she observes, a man is compelled to marry the girl whom he has seduced. This is voted equable and moral. Now, if a young man puts the marriage-ceremony before rather than after the carnal connection, surely his behaviour is even more laudable in equity and ethics ? When his spouse has made this point, Mr. B—— enters the lists with a rambling disquisition which presumably is meant to prove that Pamela's amazing qualities are such that her career cannot be held to create a precedent in any respect. The company bestow the same applause on his reasoning as on Pamela's. Richardson contrives, not uncharacteristically, to " have it both ways ": it is just and proper for young men to marry their mothers' maids ; it is doubtfully just and proper for them to do so, since the example of so exceptional a person as Pamela proves nothing.

70

One may note, too, in concluding a consideration of
Pamela in her Exalted Condition, that in it are mentioned
two characters absent from the earlier story, who were
to play important parts in Fielding's *Joseph Andrews*,
namely Mr. Adams, Pamela's chaplain, to whom she pays
the princely stipend of £21 *per annum*, and Mr. Pounce,
" an infamous jobber or broker of stocks, marriages, or
anything," a character originally found in Steele's play of
The Tender Husband, which Pamela criticizes in her letters,
as she criticizes Locke's *Treatise on Education* and (to
M. Rousseau's approval) Ambrose Philips's *Distrest
Mother*.

About *Joseph Andrews* itself not much need be said
here.   It was not a detailed and direct criticism of *Pamela*
as *Shamela* had been.   All that Fielding does in this
book (as far as *Pamela* is concerned) is to tell a story in
which certain of the characters first introduced by Richardson appear again and are presented in a different light—
e.g. Mr. B(ooby) and his wife Pamela and Mr. Adams—
and in which the cardinal situation of the earlier novel
recurs in an ingenious variation.   By that ingenuity it is
made to appear, actually if indefensibly, more than ever
ridiculous.   This varied situation is constituted by the
amorous advances of Lady Booby (Mr. Booby's sister-in-
law) to her footman, Joseph Andrews, Pamela's brother,
and by the spirited defence of his manly virtue which he
puts up in emulation of his sister's great example.   This,
however, is only one factor in an elaborate and intricate
intrigue.   For the rest, a few sly and not very important
thrusts apart, Fielding here contents himself with what
has been called " the essence of revenge ; " in no way,
neither in fable, technique, outlook nor style, does he
agree to " be like " his great rival.

SAMUEL RICHARDSON

§ 5

Mrs. Barbauld very properly called *Pamela in her Exalted Condition* "less a continuation than the author's defence of himself." It must have seemed to Richardson that he had recklessly started out to correct morals with the useful aid of art and had then found not only every article of his teaching meticulously scrutinized, but some of them even shown to be of questionable value. *Pamela, Part II* had perhaps put some of them in a better light, but there were many things in the original story that could not be altered or explained away. He was resolved that no such weaknesses should appear in his next work : he spent years instead of months over its composition and submitted it to several friends for judgment before the final revision and publication. His labours and cares were abundantly rewarded.

The title-page of *Clarissa*, " a Piece from first to last, that owes its Being to Invention," runs as follows :

Clarissa, or, the History of a Young Lady : Comprehending The most Important Concerns of Private Life. And particularly shewing, The Distresses that may attend the Misconduct Both of Parents and Children, In Relation to Marriage. Published by the Editor of Pamela.

This is the story :

While paying court to Miss Arabella Harlowe, a member of a family of well-to-do country gentry, the brilliant Mr. Robert Lovelace finds himself more strongly attracted by her younger sister, Clarissa, and transfers his attentions to her. This enhances the family ill-will towards Clarissa, already sufficiently provoked at a special legacy devised by her grandfather to her. Her brother James, mortified by the ill-success of an encounter which, on his own provocation, he has had with Lovelace, and reinforced by slighted Arabella, consequently has little difficulty in representing to the Harlowe family council that, as Mr. Lovelace's character and past are alike scandalous, his courtship of Clarissa, even if it be " honourable," is fraught with danger to the family name and that, to free them of all responsibility for her actions, she should forthwith be married to her declared suitor, Roger Solmes. The Harlowes, stiffened by Clarissa's dislike of Solmes, to whom she declares she prefers death in any shape, determine to stick at nothing in carrying through the match, though, in order to keep the redoubtable Lovelace quiet and unsuspecting, they pusillanimously connive at Clarissa's continued correspondence with him. He finds no difficulty then in representing himself to her as her only ally in her desperate struggle to avoid Solmes and, with the help of a pre-arranged trick, gets her to elope with him. This finally and completely alienates her from her family.

Once Lovelace has Clarissa in his power—as he may now be said to have—he experiences a conflict in his mind between his love for her and his wish, quickened by opportunity, to humble the proud Harlowes who have treated him so badly. The issue is decided by a sadistic pride which urges him, as has been his practice in similar affairs before, to have her on his own terms, that is, to enjoy her as his mistress before making her his wife. Clarissa is much too proud herself to bring him to the point of proposing marriage to her, when he palpably holds back, or to force the few vague openings in that direction which he

SAMUEL RICHARDSON

gives her. He settles her in an establishment in London, kept by Mrs. Sinclair and described as a private brothel, introduces her to male and female rakes and, after one unsuccessful attempt upon her honour during a pretended outbreak of fire, violates her when she is under the influence of an opiate, administered at Mrs. Sinclair's suggestion to weaken her resistance.

When Clarissa emerges from her stupor and recollects what at the time she but dimly perceived to be happening to her, she loses her reason for a time and then subsides into melancholia. Lovelace, overcome by remorse and galled by the scorn and reproaches of his confidant Belford, offers her marriage. Clarissa refuses point-blank and maintains that attitude unswerving, even when Lovelace's relations beg her to honour their family by joining it. With much presence of mind, she frees herself from Mrs. Sinclair's establishment and moves into rooms off Bow Street, where Belford takes her under his (honourable) protection. Her health, impaired already by the excitement of her elopement, now breaks down and, after elaborate preparations both of the material and spiritual order, she dies before her cousin and trustee, Colonel Morden, unhappily abroad during the earlier course of events narrated, can bring about a reconciliation between her and her somewhat softened family. Though expressly enjoined by her to eschew revenge, Morden challenges Lovelace and mortally wounds him in a duel fought at Trent in Italy.

§ 6

Like *Pamela*, *Clarissa*, an organism come alive in the imagination, does many things which its begetter never

74

intended or saw. It was meant to teach, it did teach and, of a surety, it still continues to teach, but by no means the lessons that Richardson had at heart and which he specified in the Preface to the first and the Postscript to the last volume. His chief aim, these pronouncements tell us, was not a delineation of English manners in his own time, animated by the story of an elopement, not the portrayal of a fine character superficially humiliated while inwardly preserving and enhancing its dignity, but an exposition, artfully disguised, of the " *highest and most important doctrines of Christianity* "—no less.

A sympathetic reader of to-day, confining his attention to the story alone, would conclude that Richardson proposed to himself a lay sermon on the text " the Kingdom of God is within you " and might go on to applaud him for his exemplification of this sublime theme. But a subsequent investigation of the Preface and Postscript would disabuse him. Richardson's doctrines keep much closer to earth. Indeed, the only religious one which he singles out with any particularity is first cousin to that which had exposed him to the criticisms and other annoyances of *Pamela*, the " doctrine of *future rewards*." As the design of the story was serially unfolded, many readers (among whom one is surprised to note Fielding) demanded that the disaster which they saw impending over Clarissa might be averted, that " poetic justice " should in the end be done her to the tune of wedding-bells : in fact, they wanted Virtue Rewarded almost exactly as had been done in *Pamela*. It is highly to Richardson's honour as an artist that he never dreamed, as Dickens or Trollope would have done in a sweeter age, of giving way to this clamour and committing his old blunder in its old form again. Speaking of himself in the third person, he says :

SAMUEL RICHARDSON

" He always thought that *sudden conversions*, such, especially, as were left to the candour of the reader to *suppose* and *make out*, had neither *art*, nor *nature*, nor even *probability*, in them ; and that they were moreover of very *bad* example. To have a Lovelace, for a series of years, glory in his wickedness, and think that he had nothing to do, but as an act of grace and favour to hold out his hand to receive that of the best of women, whenever he pleased, and have it thought that marriage would be a sufficient amends for all his enormities to others as well as to her—he could not bear that."

That is excellent. Curiously enough, however, he did not discern that, by insisting on the sanctity in which Clarissa died and on the corollary that her behaviour under trial had won her the passport to paradise, he was in effect merely post-dating the Reward and paying it in a different currency from that in common use at B—— Hall. He substituted a transcendental for a sublunary audit : and that was all. Many of the ethical objections to *Pamela*, therefore, may be urged against *Clarissa* too.

The real effectiveness, indeed, of the novel and its true ethical significance lie in the precise opposite of this notion, in that sublime outcry of Clarissa's in which the story culminates : " *The man who has been the villain to me that you have been shall never make me his wife.*" It is the irrevocability of human action that *Clarissa* inculcates, the stern truth that no reparation is possible to cancel out selfish cruelty, wantonly devised to give the maximum of anguish. As ruthlessly as Hebbel or Ibsen he shows how unpardonable is the sin of violating personality. After Lovelace's outrage Clarissa Harlowe has, in her opinion, lost everything that might give human

life a meaning for her ; whether this opinion of hers be
" right " or " wrong " matters nothing at all ; she is
adult and has a full right to her own values, since she is
staking her life on their validity. Nothing that Lovelace
or anyone else can do can wipe out the vital bankruptcy
which he has brought upon her ; death is nothing now to
her : in the cant of every day, it is a release.

Richardson, in fine, would seem to be far out in his
general estimate of his own work. Not only does he
miss the true point of his own doctrine, but he is incon-
sistent in what he would have us accept in its place,
Having disposed of poetic justice with great vigour and
copious quotations from Addison, Aristotle, Horace,
Rapin, etc., he decides, very much as he did over a certain
point in *Pamela, Part II,* to have his cake as well as eat
it and explains to the patient reader that after all, in spite
of his arguments, poetic justice *is* done in this narrative :

" For, is not Mr. Lovelace, who could persevere in
his villanous views, against the strongest and most frequent
convictions and remorses that ever were sent to awaken
and reclaim a wicked man—is not this great, this *wilful*
transgressor, condignly *punished* ; . . . is not Mr. Belton,
who has an uncle's *hastened* death to answer for—are not
the *whole* Harlowe family—is not the vile Tomlinson—
are not the infamous Sinclair and her *wretched partners*—
and even the wicked *servants,* who, with their eyes open,
contributed their parts to the carrying on of the vile
schemes of their respective principals— *are they not all
likewise exemplarily punished ?*

On the other hand, is not Miss HOWE, for her noble
friendship to the exalted lady in her calamities—is not
Mr. HICKMAN, for his unexceptionable morals, and

integrity of life—is not the repentant and not ungenerous BELFORD—is not the worthy NORTON—*made signally happy ? "*

Two further points of morals connected with *Clarissa* still present themselves. The first of these fills the reader with as much distrust of the author's speculative and reasoning faculties as his mutually destructive argumentations about poetic justice or his determination that Mr. B——'s notions on polygamy shall receive serious consideration and reproof. That point is his insistence that *Clarissa* gains, from the ethical and edificatory point of view, by Lovelace's avowed adherence to the tenets of Christianity. When this fine gentleman's boon-companion boasts that himself and Lovelace " are not atheists, except in *practice*," one may afford a hearty laugh at his naïve humour, while wishing that he had displayed it oftener ; but a more uneasy sensation obtrudes itself when a similar rake in *Grandison*, Sir Hargrave Pollexfen, uses almost the same language, exclaiming : " Thank God, I am a Christian in belief, though I have often been a devil in practice," and when Richardson in all the solemnity of his Preface himself declares :

" But here it will be proper to observe, for the sake of such as may apprehend hurt to the morals of youth from the more freely-written letters, that the gentlemen, though professed libertines as to the female sex, and making it one of their wicked maxims, to keep no faith with any of the individuals of it who are thrown into their power, are not, however, either infidels or scoffers ; nor yet such as think themselves freed from the observance of those other moral duties which bind man to man."

Surely such a defence of limited-liability blackguardism, such a degrading of good works below faith, of the spirit below the letter of belief, was the most dangerous, not to say criminally foolish, policy for a *vulgarisateur* of Christian ethics and a practical moral reformer, as Richardson set up to be, to bring forward !

The other point will perhaps, in an age concerned about the rights of the younger generation, arouse more curiosity than the others. The title-page promises the reader that he should witness " the Distresses that may attend the Misconduct Both *of Parents* and Children, in Relation to Marriage." The calamities that befell Clarissa need no further rehearsal. But what kind of Distresses attended the Harlowes ? Was the mere loss of a daughter, whom they had driven into misfortune and about whose welfare, while she was still alive and acutely in want of help, they apparently did not care a row of pins, to be deemed sufficient warning to tyrannical matchmakers and intriguing cowards such as them ?—equivalent, indeed, to the dishonour and death of their victim ?

Fortunately Mr. Belford, in his Conclusion, is explicit on this point :

" How did they," he exclaims about the family, " in a manner adore her memory ! How did they recriminate upon each other ! when they found, that she had not only preserved herself from repeated outrage, by the most glorious and intrepid behaviour, in defiance, and to the utter confusion of all his libertine notions, but had the fortitude, constantly, and with a noble disdain, to reject him. . . .

These intelligences and recollections were perpetual subjects of recrimination to them : heightened their anguish . . . and not seldom made them shun each other (at the times they were accustomed to meet together), that they might avoid the mutual reproaches of eyes that spoke, when tongues were silent—their stings also sharpened by time ! What an unhappy family was this ! . .

Mrs. Harlowe lived about two and a half years after the lamented death of her CLARISSA. Mr. HARLOWE had the additional affliction to survive this lady about half a year. . . . Mr. JAMES HARLOWE married a woman of family, an orphan ; and is obliged, at a very great expense, to support his claim to estates which were his principal inducement to make his addresses to her. . . . One month in every year he puts on mourning, and that month commences with him the 7th of September [the anniversary of his sister's death], during which he shuts himself up from all company. . . .

ARABELLA's fortune became a temptation to a man of quality to make his addresses to her : . . . for some years past, they have so heartily hated each other, that if either knows a joy, it is in being told of some new misfortune or displeasure that happens to the other. . . . May the reports that are spread of this lady's farther unhappiness from her lord's free life . . . be utterly groundless . . . [Clarissa's uncles] Mr. ANTONY and Mr. JOHN HARLOWE are still (at the writing of this) living : but often declare that, with their beloved niece, they lost all the joy of their lives : and lament in all companies, the unnatural part they were induced to take against her."

The President of the Immortals must have smiled a grim smile at the thought that his hand was seen in this accumulation of catastrophes. But earnest and clear-sighted observers of domestic tyranny did not smile. The elder Mrs. Chapone, undeterred by her mentor's pontificating, delivered a tremendous attack on the whole doctrine implicit in this inequality of consequences and went so far as to anticipate in the realm of family politics a celebrated dictum of Burke's : that in a dispute between rulers and ruled, the former are always directly or indirectly in the wrong. Richardson had decidedly the worst of the argument, but naturally affected not to see it.

§ 7

None of these serious criticisms was made publicly while *Clarissa* was a topic of general discussion. It seems indeed a trifle odd that an age and a nation preponderantly concerned with the didactic aspect of art paid so little attention to the major ethical considerations which attentive reading of *Clarissa* must have raised. No doubt, then as now, ninety-nine novel-readers out of a hundred did not read attentively ; on the other hand, the specialists in ethics—and as such we may fitly describe the Anglican bishops and other theologians of the eighteenth century—either read no fiction or considered it beneath their dignity to enter into public debate with writers of it. So it was, in the main, left to the minor morality-mongers to vent their criticism on *Clarissa*, which they did much more ineffectively than *Pamela* had been scrutinized.

Many of their objections, of which one finds isolated echoes in the memoirs and correspondences of the age, were collected in an anonymous and undated octavo volume of no great size called *Remarks on Clarissa*, a kind of Platonic symposium, in which the points criticized are so trifling and so easily controverted, that, as has been hinted above, one may suspect it of being part of the author's "publicity." Clarissa, we are told, for instance, lacked delicacy : first in eloping with Lovelace at all and then in seeking an interview with him after the rape. The former objection is substantial, but to bring it forwards *as an objection* to the book argues complete imbecility in the objector. For is not Clarissa's giving way to Lovelace in this one particular her *hamartia*, the tragic frailty which is so terribly visited upon her and upon which her whole history turns ? The second objection on the score of indelicacy is more obviously trivial : at the stage in the story when the alleged indecency took place Clarissa and her audience are as far above considerations of good taste and bad taste as Hamlet was above the rules of the Danish Lord Chamberlain when he appeared before the latter's daughter insufficiently gartered.

An objection of like nature which, however, the author of the *Remarks* does not make, though it rumbles about most contemporary comment as counterpart to the chief accusation against *Pamela*, envisages the realism and lusciousness with which, not Lovelace's successful outrage upon Clarissa (which Richardson leaves to the imagination,) but his frustrated attempt during the pretended fire at Mrs. Sinclair's house is described. Edward Moore, the author of *The Gamester*, in a distressingly blunt fashion cast even more thorough-going doubts on the sexual teaching of the book. "I am ordered," he says—and to make matters worse indicates that the order emanates from women, "I am ordered to ask the Author if he has not intended to revive the Custom of ravishing ? For it is the Opinion of some People . . . that most Men would be Lovelace's on this Point, if every Woman was as easily to be got rid of as a Clarissa." Needless to say, no shocking comments of this kind were made public either. The author of the *Remarks* preferred to fill up his puerile debate with a cavil at Clarissa's excessively religious talk, which bordered on "canting" and could only bring true devotion into disrepute. The point was raised again, and more aptly, over *Grandison*.

Criticism of non-ethical matters is equally meagre. The author was charged with coining new words and reforming the spelling of old ones. Mrs. Montagu, with others, thought that "it wants two of the greatest merits of a narrative, elegance and brevity," to the latter of which objections a young lady quoted in *Remarks on Clarissa* pertinently observes that, if laconic style be a criterion, then almanack-makers are the best historians. Strangely enough the most irritating *longueurs* to present-day tastes, those attending the unconscionable time Clarissa takes a-dying, were not felt as such by the author's contemporaries. That, at any rate, is the inference one of Mrs. Piozzi's stories about Johnson compels us to make : " It was not the two *last*, but the two *first*, volumes of Clarissa that he prized : ' For give me a sick bed, and a dying lady (said he), and I'll be pathetick myself.' "

§ 8

The freely invented *History of Sir Charles Grandison, In a Series of Letters Published from the Originals, By the Editor of Pamela and Clarissa*, begins with the concerns of Sir Charles's future wife, Miss Harriet Byron, an orphan. She is staying in London with relations, when one of her many admirers, Sir Hargrave Pollexfen (an early specimen of the bold, bad baronet ridiculed in Gilbert's *Ruddigore*), cuts her off from her party at a masquerade and essays to marry her by force. Thwarted at the first attempt, he hopes to fare better with a change of venue. But as he and his gagged victim are crossing Hounslow Heath, the latter manages to utter a cry of distress ; it is happily heard in a passing carriage, whose occupant leaps out, brushes aside furious Sir Hargrave, displacing three of his fore-teeth, and takes the distressed fair forthwith to the house of his married sister. The rescuer is another baronet, Sir Charles Grandison, and before her long stay with his relations has well begun, within three weeks in fact, Harriet is in love with him and, five weeks later, concludes to her satisfaction that her affections are reciprocated.

Unhappily, however, there is an obstacle. On a tour in Italy, undertaken before he succeeded to his title, Sir Charles Grandison had attracted the Lady Clementina, only daughter to the Marquis and Marchioness della Porretta. Pride of birth and faith had hitherto prevented the lady's parents from proposing an alliance, but the persistent lunacy of their daughter, which only her beloved's presence seemed able to dispel, now bids them discard all scruples and summon him again to Bologna. On the very day that Harriet becomes aware of Sir Charles Grandison's love for her, he sets out for Italy, accompanied by an English surgeon, Mr. Lowther, who has not only primed himself with all the available English lore on lunacy, but is also to try his skill on the wounds of Jeronymo della Porretta, Clementina's brother. Mr. Lowther proves highly successful in psychiatry and bandaging : both his patients recover to admiration and the settlement of the brooding marriage-problem becomes urgent. Sir Charles, acutely conscious of his humane obligations towards his friends the Porrettas, shows himself as accommodating as he can : he agrees even to having his daughters brought up in the superstitions of Rome, but firmly refuses to change his own faith, while the distracted Clementina proves equally recalcitrant over marrying a heretic. The hymeneal negotiations accordingly break down and, after a trying absence of nearly five months, Sir Charles is able to return to England and his love, whom he marries two months later.

Three months after the wedding a diversion in the pious placidity of the Grandison household is occasioned by the irruption of the unhappy Clementina della Porretta, fleeing from her family : they will not let her take monastic vows as she craves to do, but wish her to marry the Count de Belvedere. Her family and suitor soon following in her wake, Sir Charles is able to display his vast diplomatic skill in drawing up a treaty satisfactory to all parties, whereupon he, his wife and his all-but-bride enter into a solemn triple entente of eternal friendship on a spot in his extensive grounds which Sir Charles proposes to sanctify by the erection of a temple.

The episodes in this book are, for the most part, concerned with Sir Charles's good works—peacemaking among his friends, the provision of wives for his uncles and of a husband for his *difficile* sister Charlotte together with the conversion of the not-too-sinful ; his irresistible charm is further demonstrated by the timid love borne him by his fourteen-year-old ward, Emily Jervois.

§ 9

The central "situation" of *Grandison* has much in common with the triangle Swift-Stella-Vanessa, which had then recently become public. But its germ, its inspiration were clearly the same as had bred *Pamela* and *Clarissa*. Once more the public was to be regaled and edified by an exhibition of triumphant Virtue. But Richardson, whose tenderness towards public opinion had a counterpart in a readiness to learn from the mistakes brought home to him, was above everything resolved to forestall strictures such as had been uttered against his two firstlings. This negative element in his programme predominated and determined the peculiar character of the whole work. In place of attempted rape in *Pamela* and both attempted and actual rape in *Clarissa*, presented with great verisimilitude, the pages of *Grandison* are coloured with nothing more deleterious to the imagination than an unsuccessful attempt at a forced, though perfectly lawful marriage, and an abduction in which decorum is completely preserved ; misalliance and no alliance are replaced by a marriage of true minds, similar rank and hearts of equal temperature. There are no depraved characters like Mesdames Jewkes and Sinclair, merely an old rip of an uncle or two. Instead of dragon-like guardians whom *Polly Honeycombe* tried to turn into a proverbial expression, " as rude as the Harlowes," we have the polish of the Selbys and their affectionate kindness for the orphan Harriet. The complications of the plot are caused not by that most equivocal motor of human activity, the passions, but by divided benevolence and incompatible loyalties of an exalted order, and the great heartbreak of the story, Clementina's, is the consequence of honourable religious scruples, whose reconciliation has vainly exercised some of the wisest heads and kindest hearts of centuries. Richardson freed himself too of the terrible moral difficulties involved in the Reward of Virtue.

Here no single Virtuous act is, actually or by implication, confronted with a Vicious alternative, and no specified recompense directly follows on the first, no punishment on the second. The main characters never leave the plane of Virtue, so to speak, or stand in any danger of being forced from it. Virtue simply brings with it an increment of Virtue.

Lastly, Richardson extended to his artistry the improvements which were, if possible, to exalt *Sir Charles Grandison* above his earlier work. *Clarissa* had been accused of being too long, too prolix in its style, too solemn, even where solemnity was not essential. Though there are actually more situations, more things to write about, in *Grandison* than in *Clarissa*, it does not run to quite its length ; the letters that convey the story are shorter, brisker, more sprightly ; Harriet Byron has a lightness of touch foreign to the simple ignorant piety of Pamela Andrews and to tragic Clarissa Harlowe, and even the Good Man himself makes an occasional essay at jocularity (with rather disastrous results) ; again a sub-plot is introduced to leaven the whole, but it revolves about a much gayer person even than Anna Howe, namely Charlotte Grandison. In this way *Grandison* actually contrived to make converts for the author, such as Edward Young's noble friend, the Duchess of Portland, who had hitherto remained obdurate.

But the critics were not altogether silenced, though their objections were fairly mild and, once more, chiefly concerned with questions of behaviour. It was again said that the many " *sweet blessed Words* would better become an old Nurse than any of the Parties that use them,"—indeed, the same writer stigmatized good little Emily Jervois as " little better than a Driveller ; " but naturally the main focus of comment was the religious, or rather confessional, problem raised by the contemplated alliance between the Anglican Sir Charles and the Papist Clementina.

In one sense the mildest reproof administered by the champions of orthodoxy was that directed against the hero's omission to consult his father (then still alive) when the possibility of an alliance with the Porrettas first presented itself ; as this accused Grandison of filial neglect, the censure probably disconcerted the author, that great stickler for the domestic proprieties, disproportionately much. The main issue, however, obscured the other and, causing widespread discussion, called forth a defence from the author in the form of a " Reply to a Gentleman, who had objected to Sir Charles's offer'd Compromise in the Article of Religion," appended to the second and later editions of the novel, as well as to the *Collection of Sentiments*. For once, Richardson did not set out to prove too much and the arguments with which he disposed of the Gentleman could hardly be bettered :

(*i*) the Church of England envisages the possibility of salvation outside its pale, so any laxness it shows in allowing mixed marriages need not prove spiritually calamitous.

(*ii*) Sir Charles acted under the influence of passion and pity for the distracted Clementina when he thought of marrying her. When able to judge more coolly he condemned his own conduct.

(*iii*) All marriage-treaties involve concessions.

(*iv*) In reserving the males of the union for the Church of England Grandison exacted a greater sacrifice really than he made.

Aiter such niggling it is a relief to come to something like criticism in Joseph Warton's stupendous encomium :

" But of all the representations of madness, that of Clementina, in the History of Sir Charles Grandison, is the most deeply interesting. I know not whether even the madness of Lear is expressed by so many little strokes of nature and genuine passion. Shall I say it is pedantry to prefer and compare the madness of Orestes, in Euripides, to that of Clementina ? "

As a whole, however, for all its " improvements " and moral inassailability, *Grandison* must be held a poorer thing than *Clarissa* or the original *Pamela*. Richardson's preoccupation with the debit side of his last account caused him to neglect the other. If *Grandison* offends the fastidious less than its predecessors, it equally gives less general delight.

Chapter Four

RICHARDSON'S ART

§ 1

The form which Richardson adopted for the telling of *Pamela* is directly indicated on the title-page. It is "a Series of Familiar Letters." The "convention" underlying this word—as a "convention" of some sort must be assumed for all novels—is then an almost purely documentary one. Richardson places himself in the position of an editor, arranging and publishing without comment a series of thirty-two letters from Pamela to her parents, followed by a long Journal which Pamela herself wrote while cut off from her friends at B—— Hall and which she intended at some time to communicate to her father and mother : this Journal embraces, beside some verse, also copies of a number of letters, some written by Pamela, others to her, others again which fall into neither of these classes. In the break between the letter-half and the journal-half of the book the Editor in his own person gives an account of the heroine's transportation from Bedfordshire to Lincolnshire (garnished, by the way, with two letters), ending after a fashion to become excessively popular : "We shall now leave the honest old pair, etc." In the same way, at the conclusion of the semi-epistolary Journal, the Editor again chimes in, when he proceeds to step aside from his heap of alleged documents

and to deliver a brief homily on the moral lesson which
they may afford. With *Pamela, Part II* Richardson
refined the epistolary novel by rejecting utterly anything
in the way of a Journal or Memoir.

The technique of *Clarissa* (like that of *Grandison*
afterwards) is the same, though more elaborate. Again
we have the vast bulk of the work occupied by a series of
correspondences, comprising no less than five hundred
and forty-seven letters, a figure which does not include
others quoted wholly or in part in other letters. But
whereas in the original *Pamela* the documents without
exception all pass either from or to the heroine, *Clarissa*
has two epistolary focuses in the heroine and hero. Most
of wnat Clarissa herself experiences appears from letters
written by her to her friend, Miss Anna Howe, who, in
her turn, has something of a romance, if a very mild one,
to relate in her replies, namely her wooing by the worthy,
if dull, Mr. Hickman, which proceeds so very differently
from the tragic courting of Clarissa. Lovelace tells his
side of the story in a correspondence with Mr. Belford,
who begins by being his copesmate and is reformed by the
scenes which, directly and indirectly, he witnesses.

It may be noted that, although very many letters pass
from Clarissa and Lovelace to others than their corres-
pondents-in-chief, there are only two directly exchanged
between the principals themselves, though quotations from
such and summaries abound in other documents. The ama-
teur of love-letters accordingly will find little here. In
addition to the letters, there is some slight " editorial
matter," the observation, for instance, that at one point
in the story " Mr. Lovelace lays himself under a curse too
shocking to be repeated," but notably the fairly lengthy
" Conclusion supposed to be written by Mr. Belford,"

which, as we saw in the last chapter, recounts the later history (and, in one or two instances, the antecedents too) of the minor characters figuring in the main narrative. In passing, one may point out that in *Clarissa*, while maintaining his old " device," Richardson gave up the pretence of serving merely as Editor. He refers to himself as " the Author " and honestly advertises the Conclusion as *supposed* to be written by Mr. Belford.

§ 2

Prima facie it would seem hard to find a story-telling device that more perfectly gave the impression of actuality than the letter-form which Richardson chose. It cuts off before utterance all awkward questions about author's omniscience and avoids the over-simplification of motives in the interest of subsequent developments. As it encourages wastefulness, so it excuses all clumsiness of procedure, since something approximating a chronological order has to be observed and time is not concerned to give human activities a harmonious pattern.

But to these general advantages of the epistolary method came some particularly convenient to Richardson. First and foremost, it was his one and only natural form of self-expression. Later eighteenth-century gossip indeed reported so great a passion for letter-writing in him, that he used to communicate in that way with his own daughters when they were all living under the same roof together. Moreover, letter-writing served as his introduction to those aspects of life which most profoundly stirred the artist within him. It is related of him how, when he was a boy, certain young women of the neighbourhood in which he lived, conceiving a high opinion of his discretion and penmanship, used to employ him to write their love-letters for them when they were in distress, whereby he acquired not only insight into many of the forms which amatory passion assumes and induces, but also into those *détours* of thought and expression which the semi-publicity of the proceeding encouraged. The latter fact, in an apprisement of Richardson's genius, is as important as the former. Lastly, his reputation for dedicatory epistles and the like brought him his commission for the *Familiar Letters* ; his success there in telling stories, inculcating doctrine and indicating minds at issue encouraged him to write *Pamela* in the way which this success made the obvious one ; and, after the acclamation of *Pamela*, it would have needed a much younger man, a man more self-assured and interested in the processes of art than Richardson was, to experiment with any radically new technique.

The letter-form, as newly perfected, was at once subjected to careful consideration by so competent a judge as Fielding, one of the best-read men of his age as well as a practising novelist, who, in a preface to his sister Sarah's *Familiar Letters between the principal characters in David Simple* (1747) delivered it as his opinion, somewhat pontifically, that : " No one will contend that the epistolary style is in general the most proper to a novelist, or that it hath been used by the best writers of this kind." To this Richardson retorted in the postscript to *Clarissa* next year with some acerbity, but no less justice :

" Some have wished that the story had been told in the usual narrative way of telling stories. . . . The author thinks he ought not to prescribe to the taste of others ; but imagined himself at liberty to follow his own. He

SAMUEL RICHARDSON

perhaps mistrusted his talents for the narrative kind of writing. He had the good fortune to succeed in the epistolary way once before."

Although a series of chances imposed on Richardson his method of conveying a story, he was fully conscious of its great advantages. Since he worked from day to day without any detailed plan and, like his Pamela, found it morally impossible to indite a short letter, prolixity was inevitable ; besides, " there was frequently a necessity to be very circumstantial and minute, in order to maintain that air of probability, which is necessary to be maintained in a story designed to represent real life ; " he himself, as an author, might have a literary reputation to keep up,— but surely his characters, whose words, as Editor, he merely had to transcribe, might be as devious and " low " as they liked ! Most important of all, the letter-form gave scope, such as perhaps no other method and certainly not the obvious alternative of plain narrative in the third person would have afforded, for Richardson's amplest and most valuable gift, his faculty of picturing the soul as it flies.

" All the letters," he remarks in the Preface to *Clarissa*, " are written while the hearts of the writers must be supposed to be wholly engaged in their subjects (the events at the time generally dubious) : so that they abound not only with critical situations, but with what may be called *instantaneous* descriptions and reflections."

" The nature of familiar letters," he says elsewhere, " written, as it were, to the *moment*, when the heart is agitated by hopes and fears, on events undecided, must plead an excuse for the bulk of a collection of this kind.

More facts and characters might be comprised in a much
smaller compass : but would they be equally interesting ? "

This method naturally has its drawbacks, of which
there is pragmatic proof in its complete neglect by the best
novelists since Dostoïevsky completed *Poor People* over
eighty years ago. Its main justification may be its realism,
yet in successful practice it presupposes a cardinal improbability, namely that all the correspondents must possess
something like the same literary ability as their " editor "
or author and yet remain, at the same time, men and
women of action. If nothing happens to them to write
about, no amount of realism and technical skill can make
their writing interesting. If, on the other hand, they
live in a whirl of experiences, the reader finds it hard to
account for the regularity with which their experiences
are retailed. He is strongly inclined to resent their
literary activity as essentially " bookish."

Richardson cleverly devised long periods of captivity or
semi-captivity to allow for, nay encourage, some of his
chief correspondents' prolixity. But of the bookishness
which a good novel in the letter-form almost requires
there are abundant examples in the work of its perfecter.
The characters consistently view the situations in which
they or their friends find themselves, not so much as
personal experience, as " copy " in the journalist's sense
of the word. Almost all that Mrs. Howe, the mother
of Clarissa's staunchest friend, can suggest in her terrible
predicament is that she should make a book of it ! In
order to keep the story going upon the lines decreed for it,
many of the characters have to behave like a diplomatist
whose sole care is the inviolability of his mails. Directly
Clarissa, for instance, realizes that her family threaten her

freedom, her first concern is to make caches of pens, ink and paper in convenient places ; and such is her preoccupation with these commodities that, later, when she falls into delirium, her unconscious self clamours for them like a manual of French conversation. And, of course a veritable *cacoethes scribendi* assails, like an epidemic, all the major characters (except poor Mr. B——, who was no doubt as sorely puzzled about writing a letter as in every other transaction of life). Harriet Byron avows herself a " scribler ; " Lovelace goes on writing letters on one knee in a damp coppice, and his friend Belford (whom one might almost describe as a rake by profession, since he has no other occupation,) will sit by a deathbed to note that " He is now at the last gasp—rattles in the throat—has a new convulsion every minute almost ! . . . His eyes look like breath-stained glass, etc." The same, in the course of his eulogy on the deceased Clarissa (who, at the crisis of her fate, spent her time making minutes about everything as it passed, until the opium did its work), sees fit to advance as his opinion " that there never was a woman so young, who wrote so much and with such celerity." She must, however, have had a dangerous rival in Pamela Andrews, whom we should probably be right, on general grounds, in qualifying as " the unlettered Pamela." *She* spends most of her wedding-day " *écrivant comme quatre*," as Nivelle de la Chaussée has it, while on the following " Tuesday morning, the sixth of my happiness," she contrives to put a matter of sixteen thousand words to paper. One doubts whether Clarissa's celerity could outstrip this ! And the ladies had not, it seems, the benefit of shorthand, in which Lovelace and Belford were inexplicably proficient and which adds a terror to eavesdroppers in *Grandison*.

A further drawback to Richardson's method is the overlapping and constant repetition which only the most careful preliminary planning could have kept within respectable limits. It is clear that, in general, when A writes to B about an event P, he will not be guided in in his account of P by what, unbeknown to himself, X may be detailing to Y about the same ; he will have to recapitulate as preliminary explanation a good deal of what he said in his last letter and, at the conclusion of his epistle, will probably not refrain from a prophecy on the probable course of events, which is as likely as not to have come wholly or partially true in time for full report in the next letter. Moreover, as Miss Thomson points out, often " we are made familiar with a fact before we are acquainted with its cause," which means more writing about it and about at a subsequent period of the story. This prolixity obscures the chronology of the works : years of time seem to elapse while the thousands of words flow past ; but, in fact, *Pamela I* is an affair of a few weeks, *Clarissa* of less than a year.

§ 3

After a consideration of the advantages and disadvantages of the " epistolary way " as such, there remains not very much to remark about Richardson's technique. The epistolary method has, clearly, much in common with the dramatic, since the characters, standing on their own feet (so to speak) and unintroduced save by one another, vent letters instead of speeches and since the action is made up of a series of " scenes," with no general summaries. Richardson and his friends recognize the affinity, the former speaking of the " History (or rather Dramatic

Narrative) of Clarissa," while Aaron Hill urged him, after his work, to embark on straightforward tragedy, a form on which he had clearly bestowed a fair amount of attention independently.

Although less cramped for space, Richardson, like the true dramatists, experienced difficulty with his "expositions." In his first letter to his faithful friend Belford, Mr. Lovelace, for instance, tells him a lot of things he must have known perfectly well before. In *Grandison*, however, Richardson achieved a perfect, almost Shakespearian opening. The first sentence of the first letter in the book, to Harriet Byron from her correspondent-in-chief, Lucy Selby, runs : " Your resolution to accompany Mrs. Reeves to London, has greatly alarmed your three lovers." These fourteen words at once put the reader in possession of the salient fact that a new chapter is about to open abruptly in the life of the attractive Miss Byron and that those which have gone before need be of no account ; it also indicates symbolically that the theme of the new chapter will be the amours of Harriet Byron.

Altogether, from the technical point of view, *Grandison* can be called Richardson's best book. With his rather jejune material he managed to make quite a good showing, largely by means of the long suspensory, retarding affair of Sir Charles Grandison's second visit to Italy, which, the reader realizes, is probably a mere episode, but may at any time inflict something not far short of disaster on the heroine. And the introduction in person of Clementina della Porretta into the falling action whips up flagging interest in the story of the heroine more efficaciously than the similarly retarded appearance of Colonel Morden at the end of *Clarissa*. Richardson learned to use such delayed entrances very well : there is no such thing in

Pamela really, since Mrs. Jewkes is but an extension of
Mr. B——s' will, not a new factor in the situation ; but
Lovelace does not come into action until page 176 of
Clarissa and the equally late entry of Sir Charles Grandison is, of course, melodramatically effectively in the best
approved style. Similarly, Richardson contrived very
cleverly to put off until 6 July a complete account of the
crisis of *Clarissa*, which had eventuated in the night from
the 12th to the 13th of June.

"Stratagem and contrivance . . . thou knowest to
be the delight of my heart," Lovelace writes to Belford.
Richardson shared this delight, loving to complicate a
potentially straightforward course of events and, in spite
of his opportunist methods of work, always knowing
exactly where all his characters—and they are pretty
numerous—were in time and space. The careful
chronology of *Clarissa* reveals no flaw, and Sir Charles
Grandison's journey to Italy with Mr. Lowther no doubt
tallies perfectly with the eighteenth-century equivalent
of the *Continental Bradshaw*.

§ 4

Two things primarily determined the nature of the
stories which Richardson had to tell in his epistolary way:
his ethical purpose and his introduction to the life of the
imagination. On the one hand, as he says explicitly in
the Preface to *Grandison*, all three books are to be taken
as a trilogy of *Virtue Triumphant* ; without exception, on
the other hand, their interest is centred on young women
in love, as had been those damsels of the time of William
and Mary who employed young Sam Richardson as their
confidential secretary ; and these young women find them-

selves all in a more or less uncomfortable, not to say desperate, situation as the consequence of their love. To synthesize : the theme of the three novels is *Harassed Virtue Triumphant.*

Now stories of the cruel stepmother and her meek, good stepdaughter, which feed the morbid fancies of the young, are all laid in fairy-land. Unless Virtue is allied to Imbecility (when it almost ceases to be Virtue,) it cannot, in the world of every day, be persecuted unhindered for long enough to make a novel. The generalization is confirmed by Richardson's practice ; for it must be owned that the general course of two at least out of his three novels is conditioned by great improbabilities, while the third, *Grandison*, only succeeds in surmounting the cardinal difficulty by minimizing both the Harassment and the Triumph.

There can be no doubt that Mr. B—— acted quite illegally in keeping Pamela deprived of her liberty at his Bedfordshire and Lincolnshire seats ; and it may be noted in passing that the historical Sir Arthur Hesilrige committed none of the illegalities detailed in the novel. Pamela herself recognized the anomaly of her position. " Is there no constable," she asks, " no head borough, though, to take me out of his house ? for I am sure I can safely swear the peace against him : But, alas ! he is greater than any constable : he is a justice himself." That may be : nevertheless, young Mr. B—— would certainly not have liked even the Verges and Dogberry of the neighbourhood to have learnt such intimate details of his private life as Pamela would have revealed in swearing the peace against him, nor can one imagine that the other Justices of the County felt too much awe of his power and attainments to interfere when the gossip or a complaint reached their ears. The main fault is made to lie in Pamela's will : she refuses to take effective action. Says the cynical Frenchman who wrote his *Lettre sur Pamela :* " Une fille qu'on veut séduire, qui en est persuadée, se résout tranquillement à rester exposée : et quel important motif la détermine ? Une veste à broder."

In *Clarissa* the circumstantial improbability is really glaring, as the divided will of the heroine need not be taken into account. For here Richardson dealt not with a (reputedly) frightened, ignorant little servant-girl of fifteen in a remote country district, but with an uncommonly mature, level-headed young lady of the same social standing as her persecutor, who made himself guilty of what was then a capital offence against her. It has often been remarked (with a certain disregard for chronological detail) what short work would have been made of Mr. Lovelace, if Clarissa Harlowe had made a deposition before her neighbour in Bow Street, Henry Fielding, J.P. But this is by no means the major objection to the story of *Clarissa*, since it may be answered validly by reference to Clarissa's natural repugnance from an odious publicity and the honourable desire she always manifested to wreak no vulgar revenge on Lovelace. The author's little friend, Sally Wescomb, though hardly more than a child, put her finger on the really weak spot when she wrote to the author : " Permit me to say, that it seems a little unnatural that so general an Infatuation shou'd run thro Clarissa's whole Family, as does not often happen, to bring about the Ruin of this admirable young Creature." The twin postulates underlying the story, (*a*) that Clarissa was a paragon of good behaviour and amiability, and (*b*) that she could be forced into the power of Lovelace and kept there in the manner described, are, indeed, incompatible with one another. Even if we allow that her brother was a complete cad, that her father and uncles were monsters of egotism and barbarous family pride, that her mother (and she a viscount's daughter, who had married into the untitled gentry !) had been utterly cowed, we cannot believe that no neighbouring family, knowing and liking Clarissa and convinced of her goodness, would have taken notice of her distress, though for no better reason than to score off so odious a set of people as her relatives, capable of complete demoralization at threats from a Lovelace. It is incredible that no friend of Anna Howe's or Mrs. Howe's, say worthy Mr. Hickman, even if reluctant to come out into the open, should have given a hint in time to some metropolitan constable or magistrate or the Secretary of State, whose time was not heavily occupied in those days.

To the main story of *Clarissa* was appended a complete sub-plot, more sketchily indicated, concerning Clarissa's friend and confidante, Anna Howe. It recalls the sub-plot of many of the sentimental comedies then coming into fashion in contrasting a sprightly heroine with a humourless one, just as long ago Shakespeare had contrasted Beatrice and Hero. It calls to mind certain Elizabethan and Restoration plays, too, in that none of the actors involved in the sub-plot ever meet those who carry on the principal action.

In *Grandison*, again, this is better managed. Since the rudimentary story revolving round the rattle Charlotte Grandison can hardly rank as such, the subsidiary plot to the Harriet-Grandison love-story is the Clementina-Grandison affair, as intimately associated with it as the Hermione-plot is with the Andromaque-plot in Racine's play which Richardson knew as *The Distrest Mother*.

The original *Pamela* had no sub-plot at all ; a cynic might, however, say that the two further volumes added to it were *all* sub-plot, at least bore no traces of a main action.

The purpose of these sub-plots was, as usual, to provide " relief," to bring new interests into play and give opportunities for further elucidating the characters of the principal personages and their circumstances and springs of action. The same may be said of those long " static " periods in the main action, most frequently occurring towards the end of the novels, though they are often filled out with mere gossip and episodes which in no wise advance the chief story. The episodes do not, however, distract attention ; they do not leave an impression on the reader's mind sharper than that left by the scenes of which the main plot is composed. There is nothing comparable in any of Richardson's works, for instance, with the marvellous scene in Marivaux's *Marianne* (not very relevant to the story) in which the abusive cab-driver meets his match in Mme. Duval. The graceful scenes of coquetry by the pond of Mr. B——'s Lincolnshire home come perhaps nearest.

§ 5

Much of Richardson's appeal, contemporary and posthumous, proceeds from the quality which above all others could find the completest scope in the kind of story he preferred. Those who deny him the power of evoking the truly Tragic in *Clarissa* have in their support weighty arguments, mostly forced upon them by the unwitting author himself—notably that insistence upon the heavenly audit. But none who consider him of the slightest account as an artist deny him his command over the Pathetic.

Here, too, the field is not limited to a single book, but is co-extensive with the sum of his imaginative writing. Pamela, Clarissa, Clementina, Harriet, with their hopeless hopes, their true merits and their hard predicaments, are, in their varying degrees, all pathetic figures, even when, as in the first instance, the pathos achieved falls something short of the pathos intended. "Pathetic figures" means of course "persons in pathetic situations," and it is almost superfluous to add that since the heroines are pathetic, pathetic situations abound. In view of Richardson's minuteness and diffuseness, which are of the essence of his method, it is impossible to exemplify the various varieties of such situations in his works. But one may and should quote, without having to fill a volume, one of the passages in which, of necessity, the pathos is concentrated and, therefore, comparatively succinct. Such passages are notably to be found in the descriptions of death-beds, of which there are several in the novels. (One of them, remarkable for the complete lack of pathos, will receive consideration in another connection.) The finest example to choose for the present purpose is the account which Mr. Belford gives of the death of Clarissa.

"The Colonel was the first that took my attention, kneeling on the side of the bed, the lady's right hand in both his, which his face covered, bathing it with his tears ; although she had been comforting him, as the women since told me, in elevated strains, but broken accents.

On the other side of the bed sat the good widow ; her face overwhelmed with tears, leaning her head against the bed's head in a most disconsolate manner ; and turning her face to me, as soon as she saw me, O Mr. Belford, cried she, with folded hands—the dear lady—a heavy sob

permitted her not to say more. Mrs. Smith, with clasped
fingers and uplifted eyes, as if imploring help from the
only Power which could give it, was kneeling down at
the bed's feet, tears in large drops trickling down her
cheeks. Her nurse was kneeling between the widow and
Mrs. Smith, her arms extended. In one hand she held
an ineffectual cordial, which she had just been offering to
her dying mistress ; her face was swollen with weeping
(though used to such scenes as this) ; and she turned her
eyes towards me, as if she called upon me by them to join
in the helpless sorrow ; a fresh stream bursting from them
as I approached the bed.

The maid of the house with her face upon her folded
arms, as she stood leaning against the wainscot, more
audibly expressed her grief than any of the others. The
lady had been silent a few minutes, and speechless, as
they thought, moving her lips without uttering a word ;
one hand, as I said, in her cousin's. But when Mrs.
Lovick, on my approach pronounced my name, Oh !
Mr. Belford, said she, with a faint inward voice, but very
distinct nevertheless— Now !—Now ! [in broken periods
she spoke]—I bless God for His Mercies to His poor
creature—all will soon be over—a few—a very few moments—will end this strife—and I shall be happy ! Com-
fort here sir—turning her head to the Colonel—com-
fort my cousin—see ! the blame-able kindness—He
would not wish me to be happy—so *soon !* Here she
stopt for two or three minutes, earnestly looking upon
him. Then resuming, My dearest cousin, said she, be
comforted—what is dying but the common lot ?—The
mortal frame may *seem* to labour—but that is all !—It is
not so hard to die as I believed it to be !—The preparation
is the difficulty—I bless God I have had time for that—

105

the rest is worse to beholders than to me !—I am all blessed hope—hope itself. She *looked* what she said, a sweet smile beaming over her countenance.

After a short silence, Once more, my dear cousin, said she but still in broken accents, commend me most dutifully to my father and mother—There she stopt. And then proceeding—To my sister, to my brother, to my uncles,—and tell them I bless them with my parting breath—for all their goodness to me—even for their displeasure, I bless them—most happy has been to me my punishment *here !*—Happy indeed ! She was silent for a few moments, lifting up her eyes, and the hand her cousin held not between his. Then, O *Death !* said she, *where is thy sting !* [the words I remember to have heard in the burial-service read over my uncle and poor Belton.] And after a pause,—*It is good for me that I was afflicted !* Words of Scripture, I suppose. Then turning towards us, who were lost in speechless sorrow. O dear, *dear* gentlemen, said she, you know not what *foretastes*, what *assurances*——And there she again stopped, and looked up, as if in a thankful rapture, sweetly smiling.

Then turning her head towards me—Do *you*, sir, tell your friend that I forgive him !—And I pray to God to forgive him !—Again pausing, and lifting up her eyes, as if praying that He would. Let him know how happily I die :—and that such as my own, I wish to be his last hour. She was again silent for a few moments : and then resuming—My sight fails me !—Your voices only—[for we both applauded her Christian, her divine frame, though in accents as broken as her own] ; and the voice of grief is alike in all. Is not this Mr. Morden's hand ? pressing one of his with that he had just let go. Which is Mr. Belford's ? holding out the other. I gave her mine.

God Almighty bless you both, said she, and make you both—in your last hour—for you *must* come to this—happy as I am.

She paused again, her breath growing shorter ; and after a few minutes—And now, my dearest cousin, give me your hand—nearer—still nearer—drawing it towards her ; and she pressed it with her dying lips—God protect you, dear, dear sir—and once more receive my best and most grateful thanks—and tell my dear Miss Howe—and vouchsafe to see, and to tell my worthy Norton—she will be one day, I fear not, though now lowly in her fortunes, a saint in heaven—tell them both that I remember them with thankful blessings in my last moments !—And pray God to give them happiness *here* for many, many years, for the sake of their friends and lovers ; and a heavenly crown *hereafter ;* and such assurances of it, as I have, through the all-satisfying merits of my blessed Redeemer.

Her sweet voice and broken periods methinks still fill my ears, and never will be out of my memory. After a short silence, in a more broken and faint accent—And you, Mr. Belford, pressing my hand, may God preserve you, and make you sensible of all your errors—you see, in me, how all ends—may *you* be—and down sunk her head upon her pillow, she fainting away, and drawing from us her hands. We thought she was then gone ; and each gave way to a violent burst of grief. But soon showing signs of returning life, our attention was again engaged; and I besought her, when a little recovered, to complete in my favour her half-pronounced blessing. She waved her hand to us both, and bowed her head six several times, as we have since recollected, as if distinguishing every person present ; not forgetting the nurse and the maid-servant;

the latter having approached the bed, weeping, as if crowding in for the divine lady's last blessing ; and she spoke faltering and inwardly. Bless—bless—bless you all—and—now—and now—[holding up her almost lifeless hands for the last time] come—oh come— Blessed Lord—JESUS ! And with these words, the last but half-pronounced, expired :—such a smile, such a charming serenity overspreading her sweet face at the instant, as seemed to manifest her eternal happiness already begun."

§ 6

On proceeding to a consideration of the persons in the stories, we are again struck at the outset by the resemblances between them, rather than by their variety : a slow, but steady development is once more discernible too. The letter-form must be held partly responsible for the former peculiarity, as has been indicated above : all the main characters must possess uncommon aptitude with the pen and, at the same time, sufficient leisure to exercise this aptitude in the intervals of the action they have to report. As a natural corollary, they must be " idle " and, with almost equal necessity, " idle rich."

As time went on, to come to the second point, Richardson raised his characters in society, as becomes immediately apparent if the *Familiar Letters* are also drawn into account. Almost all the correspondents in this volume belong—naturally enough, since they require the offices of a letter-writer—to classes below the middle line of society : they are servants, small shopkeepers and their friends. Pamela Andrews, who belongs by birth to the labouring class, is enabled to devote so much time to letter-writing, because during the major part of the original story she virtually enjoys the status of a wealthy man's kept mistress without undertaking any of its obligations. Mr. B—is a Justice of the Peace, whose sister has married a title—a typical country gentleman in fact. Clarissa Harlowe and Robert Lovelace, in the next book, are again commoners, members of the gentry, but closely related to the British aristocracy : the lady's mother was, in the first edition of the book, referred to as Lady Charlotte Harlowe, though the daughter of a viscount—an error in heraldry put right before long—while the gentleman is nephew to Lord M——. In *Grandison*, once more, the rise in the social scale is slight, but perceptible : two baronets dispute the hand of the heroine, and one of them, despite the difference of faith, is considered a suitable match for the only daughter of an Italian count.

The two features just discussed have left a permanent mark on English literature. They encouraged the aristocratic, snobbish bias which is comprehensible and pardonable enough in heroic drama and its congeners, but which the line of development particularly associated with Richardson set out to correct. It is remarkable, on cool consideration, how much of their talents good middle-class radicals of the great middle-class age, like Thackeray and Dickens and Meredith, devoted to narrations of lords, baronets, knights and their hangers-on.

§ 7

The heroine serves as the real focus of each of the stories, in the sense that it is seen through her eyes ; it is also weighed in her scales. The masculine title of *Grandison* suggests an exception, especially when it is remembered that the hero in his own person holds together the threads of Harriet Byron's and Clementina's destinies ; but the exception is more apparent than real. Sir Charles walks his path with decent unconcern : its turnings, uncertainties and latent pitfalls are only realized on marking the reaction of Harriet Byron's sensibility to them. No male English novelist was to repeat the dangerous experiment of concentrating the interest of a story on a woman before the author of *Rhoda Fleming* and *Diana of the Crossways*.

The heroines have a great deal in common, in addition to sustaining the rôle of Harassed Virtue Triumphant and the circumstance that the harassment assails them from within as well as from without. They all have youth and charm, considerable self-will and knowledge, together with a great stock of piety, according to Low Church principles. Most striking affinity of all—they all have a kind of obliquity in their moral vision, what downright Dr. Johnson meant when he complained of Clarissa : "You may observe there is always something which she prefers to truth." Truth they profess to venerate and truth (to give them their due) they speak a great deal more frequently than not, but they all command an amazing gift for making the letter of truth obscure or even strive against its spirit, for proffering a *suggestio falsi* in a half-truth or literal truth. Although Harriet Byron seems freest from this vice, it did not escape the notice of her friends : "You are an unaccountable girl ! " exclaims her future sister-in-law, "You'll tell the truth ; but not the whole truth." Their instinctive casuistry, even if often excused by their situation, must (one cannot help feeling), when revealed by a professed champion of their sex, have done women in general much disservice. It accounts, perhaps, for Mrs. Carter's lack of enthusiasm for this aspect of her friend's endeavours. Certainly, those early employers of Sam Richardson's have something to answer for.

The best instance of feminine disingenuousness is afforded by Pamela Andrews. She and the story in which she figures are, indeed, only made credible after assigning to her a horrifying endowment of imposture. Uncharitable critics, as has been seen, stigmatized it as deliberate ; but the kind and just view sees it as self-deceiving. Richardson was not completely blind to this quality in her. " I know," he makes Mr. B—— say to her, " you won't tell a downright *fib* for the world : but for *equivocation !* no Jesuit ever went beyond you." The whole book of which she is the heroine (*Part II* excepted) is a coil of spoken and unspoken equivocations, which finally conduct her to the altar, with a curtsey and thank-you to Mr. B—— and something not unlike a halo round her demure head. In a sense, this young Politician, as the author of *Shamela* called her, who has instinctively mastered Mrs. Peachum's advice that

> " by keeping men off
> You keep them on,"

whose dreams are filled with ideas of rape, but whose waking moments resound to prate about her " honour," who knows exactly how she looks most fetching while she declaims against the snares of the flesh, who manages even to deceive herself quite perfectly in this elaborate hypocrisy and to wallow in self-pity, is, as the most highly differentiated and most living, also the most successful of Richardson's character-portrayals. She is a perennial type, as Sir Arthur Pinero has shown us in the Edwardian variants of *The Mind the Paint Girl*—and about the most unpleasant there is.

But so novel was the artistic presentation at that time, that doubts were cast on her verisimilitude : the French translator of the English *Anti-Pamela* claimed to speak of the majority when he wrote of *Pamela* : " en effet on est surpris . . . d'y voir une Fille qu'on nous donne pour niaise, raisonner tantôt en Philosophe, tantôt en Théologienne ; une Fille qui a un attachement presqu'inouï pour la Vertu, et qui néanmoins est la plus grande grimacière et la plus ambitieuse personne du monde. . . En un mot, ajoute-t-on, c'est un caractère si compliqué, qu'à chaque feuille du Livre, on croit voir une autre Héroïne."

Still, there is a certain *câlinerie* about even the finished Pamela which the reader cannot disown. The following passage—a complete letter of hers—will show how far Richardson was capable of conveying this impression, together with some underlying pathos, and, at the same time, how obviously he exposed himself to the shafts of *Shamela* :

" DEAR FATHER,—Since my last, my master gave me more fine things. He called me up to my late lady's closet, and, pulling out her drawers, he gave me two suits of fine Flanders laced head-clothes, three pair of fine silk shoes, two hardly the worse, and just fit for me (for my lady had a very little foot), and the other with wrought silver buckles in them ; and several ribands and topknots of all colours ; four pair of white fine cotton stockings, and three pair of fine silk ones ; and two pair of rich stays. I was quite astonished, and unable to speak for a

while ; but yet I was inwardly ashamed to take the stockings ; for Mrs. Jervis was not there : If she had, it would
have been nothing. I believe I received them very
awkwardly ; for he smiled at my awkwardness, and said,
Don't blush, Pamela : dost think I don't know pretty
maids should wear shoes and stockings ?

I was so confounded at these words, you might have
beat me down with a feather. For you must think, there
was no answer to be made to this : So, like a fool, I was
ready to cry ; and went away courtesying and blushing, I
am sure, up to the ears ; for, though there was no harm in
what he said, yet I did not know how to take it. But I
went and told all to Mrs. Jervis, who said, God put it
into his heart to be good to me ; and I must double my
diligence. It looked to her, she said, as if he would fit
me in dress for a waiting-maid's place on Lady Davers's
own person.

But still your kind fatherly cautions came into my
head, and made all these gifts nothing near to me what
they would have been. But yet, I hope, there is no
reason ; for what good could it do him to harm such a
simple maiden as me ? Besides, to be sure no lady would
look upon him, if he should so disgrace himself. So I
will make myself easy ; and, indeed, I should never have
been otherwise, if you had not put it into my head ; for
my good, I know very well. But, may be, without these
uneasinesses to mingle with these benefits, I might be too
much puffed up : So I will conclude, all that happens is
for our good ; and God bless you, my dear father and
mother ; and I know you constantly pray for a blessing
upon me ; who am, and shall always be,

Your dutiful DAUGHTER."

113

SAMUEL RICHARDSON

Pride of place among Richardson's feminine creations
Pamela must, for all her unintended excellence, dispute
with Clarissa Harlowe, who is great according to the
measure in which she fulfils her author's intention, not
in proportion as she emancipates herself from them and
takes on a vitality of her own. Clarissa is definitely cast
in the heroic mould : " had the same soul informed a
masculine body," Lovelace rightly declares, " never would
there have been a truer hero." She has her fatal flaw,
too, as befits the tragic hero : her unwarranted trust in
Lovelace, despite the warnings of her family ; and that
tragic flaw ruins her. But her heroism is mainly passive.
She is the eighteenth century counterpart of Otway's
Monimia and Hardy's Tess Durbeyfield, elevated to
greatness by what is done to her more than by what she
does. Accordingly, it is the *process* to which the supreme
interest attaches and in which her creator's unique genius
had the fullest and happiest scope,—the development of
her character under the stress of her misfortunes, from
that of an emotionally unformed, rather colourless young
lady[1], rigorously disciplining herself by a routine of
principle, through the hardest physical and sentimental
trials, to the stoic serenity of a martyr who embraces
death like a heavenly bridegroom.

Harriet Byron, whose soul navigates less treacherous
waters than do those of those of Pamela and Clarissa,
Richardson designed as a kind of mean between them,
" or, rather, to make her what I would have supposed
Clarissa to be, had she not met with such persecutions."
Her great inferiority to her sisters results from the *ex-*

[1] Her age is not, I think, perfectly clear : but it seems more
probable than not that on her birthday, which occurs about half
way through the story, on 24 July, she becomes nineteen.

clusively passive part for which her creator has cast her : she stands always at the meeting-place of forces in equilibrium and has too much good breeding to betray the magnitude of these forces. Her soul and sensibilities seem to move as little as her body. Lady Bradshaigh's quaint criticism : " The want of life is, I think, a fault in her character," really said the last word about her.

Richardson wished no doubt to emphasize Miss Byron's ladylike passivity, her Anglo-Saxon phlegm, in order to furnish as striking a contrast as possible with the Latin passion informing her rival for Sir Charles Grandison's hand. What the former lost, not merely in vitality, but also in general favour, the other gained, and most readers applauded when Nanny Williams exclaimed :

> " In *Byron* all the softer beauties shine,
> But heav'nly *Clementina's* worth be mine."

The general preference must have been due rather to her distracting position and pathetic madness than to a precise appreciation of her personality, of which one can say little more than that it was passionate beyond the bounds of reason, but neither unbridled nor entirely preoccupied with the amatory emotions.

§ 8

Only two among Richardson's male figures of major size require further discussion, since with Mr. B——, to invert a well-known dictum, destiny is character. His fate, related already, tells us all about him that we care to know. His successor, Lovelace, however, is a most interesting person from several points of view. He again, as Pamela did, attests the rare artistic vitality of the author, in coming alive and displaying a nature quite other than that intended for him. Richardson conceived him as the embodiment of splendid sin, of the pride of life (as reproved by medieval theologians), of irresistible and pernicious fascination, the eighteenth-century Lucifer, in fact, a worthy antagonist to his paragon of virtue, Clarissa. So appalling was this conception to him, that Richardson was afraid to let it loose on the public ; but Young encouraged him with brave good sense : " 'Tis the likeness, not the morality of a character we call for." In effect, however, Lovelace assumes much less terrific proportions. He is not Lucifer, but a type as perennial and common and odious as Pamela's, that of the over-grown schoolboy : a schoolboy soaked in the lust of adolescence, intoxicated with the sense of power and of immense intellectual superiority (*soi-disant* genius) which a careful preference for the society of inferiors confers and which in his eyes invests all that he does and thinks with a sheen worthy of the best effects of Covent Garden or Drury Lane. He boasts and swaggers his way through life, animated by the example of similar scoundrels of an earlier age and unhampered by pitiful considerations like politeness, affection, thought or feeling, leaving a hideous vacuum in his trail, so that, in the end, one regards him as a mark more suitable for the weapons of a gamekeeper than the sword of Colonel Morden. The portrait of this consummate cad has never been excelled for detail, insight, and (one must add) relish in the presentation. Balzac, a connoisseur of such types, in a memorable passage on the processes of genius, held that the creation of Lovelace was by itself enough to secure his maker's immortality.

But his tinsel and flashy sayings dazzled not merely himself, but his whole age as well, which saw in him what his creator intended and more, one of the most dangerous corrupters of youth and advocates of vice. There did not, in fact, appear to be much to choose between himself and that other Bad Example, Tom Jones. So Richardson, perhaps not a little uneasy at having (in Lamb's later grandiloquence) " strengthened Vice, from the mouth of a Lovelace, with entangling sophistries and abstruse pleas against her adversary Virtue which Sedley, Villiers, and Rochester, wanted depth of libertinism sufficient to have invented," felt himself obliged to provide the antidote.

As then, in the author's own words, he "presents to the public, in SIR CHARLES GRANDISON, the example of a man acting uniformly well through a variety of trying scenes, because all his actions are regulated by one steady principle : A man of religion and virtue ; of liveliness and spirit ; accomplished and agreeable ; happy in himself, and a blessing to others," it will be of interest to consider with some particularity the ideal of principle, religion, virtue, *etcetera*, which Richardson and his public held. Outwardly fashionably attired, Sir Charles is an expert horseman (but will not have his horses' tails docked), one of the finest dancers in England and a first-class fencer, though he disapproves of duelling and is able to quote the relevant decree of the Council of Trent in support of his disapproval. On one occasion he refuses to draw his sword, which Young celebrates in the distich :

"What hast thou done ? I'm ravished at the scene
A sword *undrawn*, makes mighty Cæsar *mean*."

He possesses uncommon proficiency as a linguist, a landscape-gardener and a musician—his instrument being the organ, at which he is equal to improvising the setting to a song. An early riser, he has his day carefully planned out and divided into periods for business, reading, honourable recreation and the study of science, in which, like his spiritual kinsman, Sir Willoughby Patterne he enjoys the assistance of extensive apparatus. In all things his conscience guides him : " I live not to the world : " he declares, " I live to myself ; to the monitor within," never speaking at random and apparently able to recall but one occasion on which " I had like to have forgotten myself." It is insisted that he came to the altar without having known woman—though it must have mortified Richardson exceedingly when he was told that the ladies by no means thought this to his credit : it is amusing, however, if not startling, to hear that the spotlessness of his youth was mainly due to fear of what his tutor, the Reverend Dr. Bartlett, might do or think. None the less, the *tout ensemble* is so " enormously excellent " that a Roman Catholic bishop declares that, were Grandison " one of us," he might expect canonization. The very servants in Italy decline his tips.

All this, though it may have driven Sir Charles's sister Charlotte into almost a frenzy of irritation, the contemporary public (or at least its vocal fraction) " took " as it was " meant." Grandison had, perhaps, come near to culpable neglect in countenancing the education of his potential daughters in the faith of Rome (as described above), but, apart from that, the severest charge that could be levelled against his example was the younger Mrs. Chapone's :

" The only objection I have to his book is, that I

apprehend it will occasion the kingdom's being overrun with old maids. It will give the women an idea of perfection in a man which they never had before, the consequence of which niceness will be a single life for ninety-nine out of a hundred."

§ 9

The minor characters, as distinct from mere supernumeraries, exist, like the sub-plots in which they generally take an active part, mainly in order to provide relief. Sometimes their function may be further particularized as "sentimental relief." Such is that provided amidst Lovelace's boisterous and self-confident activity in the early stages of *Clarissa* by his "Rosebud," the innkeeper's young daughter, whom with great magnanimity he resolves to love, but not debauch ; or, in *Grandison*, by more fully sketched Emily Jervois (a younger relative of Miss Godwin in Part II of *Pamela*) whose ingenuous openness in her attachment to her guardian, Sir Charles, sets off and eases the restraint that circumstances and years of discretion impose on Harriet Byron. Emily, like Pamela, is a self-deceiver, if a genuinely innocent one, and Richardson, who loved such characters with the expert creator's love, contrived to make her figure a credible and appealing one.

Most of these secondary characters, however, do not directly reinforce the pathetic appeal of the main stories like Emily Jervois and "the Rosebud," but tend rather to set it off by contrast. They serve to lighten the tone. In this function by far the greatest success is achieved by Miss Anna Howe. Clarissa's friend is as staunch and, one may imagine, as completely sound as she, but at the

SAMUEL RICHARDSON

same time she owns a nimble intelligence, which enables
her to see herself and her surroundings in due proportion,
and a keen sense of the ridiculous, which does not even
spare (as Grandisonian propriety would demand) her
friend's relations or her own loyal and upright admirer,
Mr. Hickman.

" Here [she reports on one occasion] I was interrupted
on the honest man's account. He has been here these
two hours—courting the mother for the daughter, I
suppose—yet she wants no courting neither : 'tis well
one of us does ; else the man would have nothing but
halcyon ; and be remiss, and saucy of course.

He was going. His horses at the door. My mother
sent for me down, pretending to want to say something
to me.

Something she said when I came that signified nothing
—Evidently, for no reason called me, but to give me an
opportunity to see what a fine bow her man could make ;
and that she might wish me a good night. She knows I
am not over-ready to oblige him with my company, if I
happen to be otherwise engaged. I could not help an
air a little upon the fretful, when I found she had nothing
of moment to say to me, and when I saw her intention.

She smiled off the visible fretfulness, that the man
might go away in good humour with himself.

He bowed to the ground, and would have taken my
hand, his whip in the other. I did not like to be so com-
panioned : I withdrew my hand, but touched his elbow
with a motion, as if from his low bow I had supposed him
falling, and would have helped him up—A sad slip, it
might have been ! said I.

A mad girl ! smiled it off my mother.

He was put quite out ; took his horse-bridle, stumped back, back, back, bowing, till he run against his servant. I laughed. He mounted his horse. I mounted up stairs, after a little lecture ; and my head is so filled with him, that I must resume my intention, in hopes to divert you for a few moments."

In many ways, with her charm and robust sense, as she was foreshadowed by that " facetious young Lady " of the *Familiar Letters* who wrote a letter to her Aunt, " ridiculing her serious Lover," so in her turn Miss Howe foreshadows Elizabeth Bennett and other heroines of Miss Austen's. It is interesting to know, on the authority of the *New English Dictionary*, that she is the first person to have used that modern expression " flirt " in the sense it now bears as a noun. Compared, however, with his successor's, Richardson's brush, one might say, was a little uncertain at the edges. Neither he nor Miss Howe is instinctively certain how far she may go. Her fun is sometimes forced and grating. It got on to the nerves of Lady Mary Montagu—though, to be sure, Mrs. Montagu, as competent a judge, had no fault to find.

Infinitely more exceptionable, in this respect, are Miss Howe's counterparts in the other two novels— Charlotte Grandison and Lady Davers. Richardson makes Harriet Byron describe the former in set terms which, exemplifying both his methodical minuteness and the strangely flat effect produced by it, deserve quotation for those reasons :

" Miss Grandison is about twenty-four ; of a fine stature : she has dignity in her aspect ; and a very pene-

trating black eye, with which she does what she pleases :
her hair is black, very fine and naturally curls : she is
not fair ; but her complexion is delicate and clear, and
promises a long duration to her loveliness : her features
are generally regular : her nose is a little aquiline ; but
that is so far from being a blemish, that it gives a kind of
majesty to her other features : her teeth are white and
even : her mouth is perfectly lovely ; and a modest arch-
ness appears in her smiles, that makes one both love and
fear her, when she begins to speak.   She is finely shaped ;
and, in her air and whole appearance, perfectly genteel. . . .

She has charming spirits.   I daresay she sings well,
from the airs she now and then warbles in the gaiety of her
heart, as she goes up and down stairs : she is very polite ;
yet has a vein of raillery, that, were she *not* polite, would
give one too much apprehension for one's ease : but I
am sure she is frank, easy, and good-humoured : and, by
turning over all the just and handsome things which are
attributed to herself, to her brother's credit, she must be
equally humble and generous.

She says, she has but lately taken a very great liking to
reading : but I am ready to question what she says, when
she speaks anything that some would construe to her
disadvantage.   She pretends, that she was too volatile,
too gay, too airy, to be confined to sedentary amusements.
Her father, however, according to the genteelest and most
laudable modern education for women, had given her a
master, who taught her history and geography ; in both
which she *acknowledges* she made some progress.   In
music, she *owns* she has skill : but I am told by her maid,
who attended me by her young lady's direction, and who
delights to praise her mistress, that she reads and speaks

French and Italian ; that she writes finely ; and is greatly admired for her wit, prudence, and obligingness."

It is when she acts and speaks, however, that Charlotte Grandison becomes a person—authentic, vital, and most unpleasant. The general tenor of these doings and sayings of hers may be gauged by her behaviour on leaving the church after her marriage to Lord G—— (who, poor nobleman, did his best in a very awkward position):

" Lord G—— came in : as he was entering, Harkee, friend, said Charlotte, and put out her hand, you mistake the coach : you are not of our company.

The whole world, replied my lord, shall not now divide us. . . .

This, said Lord G——, as the coach drove on, taking one hand, and eagerly kissing it, is the hand that blessed me.

And that, said she, pushing him from her with the other, is the hand that repulses your forwardness. What came you in here for ?—Don't be silly.

He was in raptures all the way."

and in similar fashion, rather reminiscent of a fuddled hoyden on Bank Holiday evening, does she behave almost all through the story.

The lapses one deplores in Miss Howe's behaviour become the norm in Miss Grandison, whom even her creator found "intolerably playful sometimes." It is, if interpreted rationalistically, no doubt comprehensible and even pardonable as a natural reaction from the ineffably sanctimonious pomposity of her brother. For Lady Davers in *Pamela*, however, there can be no comprehension and no pardon : she is simply a titled fish-fag who bounces and scolds her way over everybody's susceptibilities and expects to be valued as a jolly, downright sort of woman with a heart of gold. One suspects that, as faulty appreciation of Lady Bradshaigh's impulsiveness went to make the character of Charlotte Grandison, a half-obliterated recollection of some of the " rattling " ladies in Dryden's, Congreve's and Cibber's comedies was embodied in Lady Davers.

§ 10

Apart from the matter of Pathos, none of the avenues hitherto traversed has led to the secret of Richardson's greatness—or distinction, if the qualification of " greatness " should be thought to beg the question at issue. Grievously hampered by his *donné*, he reveals no superlative merits as a story-teller ; he may have developed to the fullest and utilized in the most skilful fashion the unusual medium with which he is commonly associated, but that medium soon perished in the struggle for the survival of the fittest. He falls equally below the first rank in the creation of character. There is in this department none of that copiousness of output, which seems to mark the true creators of character, the Chaucers, the Shakespeares, the Tolstois ; and the few characters which are realized seem flat, insufficiently differentiated. The four full-length female portraits (as well as the three kit-cats) *are*, of course, distinguishable from one another, but the differences are obscured by a general resemblance similar to that which prevents, for instance, Kneller from ranking as a supreme portrait painter. Curiously enough —since he took so much less interest in them—Richardson succeeded rather better with his two great men, as is proved by the names of Sir Charles Grandison and of Lovelace still passing current as symbols for certain human types ; but one of them is little more than a phantasmal bogey, the wraith of a being that never really lived, and only Lovelace remains, much tarnished and rather ridiculous, but still alive and real in his basic simplicity and his superficial sophistications. Even the doctrine which Richardson had so close at heart, fails of effect : the veneration which a man may feel for the passionate conviction informing the writings of Bunyan, even when he does not share that creed, cannot be commanded by a writer capable of interpreting his own great tragedy in such paltry terms as : " Going off with a Man, is the thing I wanted most to make inexcusable."

What then remains ?   How are we to explain his high standing—not merely with the vulgar reading public of his day (though that continued for long enough to make it pretty remarkable), but with connoisseurs of literary art from the Abbé Prevost, through La Harpe and Musset, to Stevenson and Mr. Arnold Bennett ?   What major literary assets have not yet been considered ?

§ 11

A distinction must be made between two artistic faculties :—between character-drawing and psychological insight, between, on the one hand, the ability to evoke with words a character that leaves exactly the same impression on our mind as the recollection of an actual personality, and a capacity, on the other hand, for explaining and correlating the outward manifestations impinging on the sensorium in this way.   The two gifts are often confused,

SAMUEL RICHARDSON

perhaps because they are completely fused when they occur together, as, for instance, in Shakespeare and in Euripides ; but though they sometimes go together, they by no means do so of necessity. Dickens is one of the supreme character-creators in the history of literature, but as a psychologist entirely negligible. Henry James, to take the opposite extreme, lays bare with unexcelled dexterity every movement of the soul which he is studying; but he has created no single character of even the rank of Cousin Feenix. And the British people, who can with justifiable pride point to the marvellous collection of great characters which their writers have created, should not, on that account, plume themselves or praise their men of letters for any singularly searching insight into the mind of man ; for the facts do not permit them justly to do so. Compared, for instance, with French literature (which is not over-strong in " character-creations "), English literature is rather deficient in the specifically psychological elements. It is all the more remarkable that by birth, unbringing and prejudice one of the most English of Englishmen, Richardson, should possess in a degree exceeded by none of his compatriots the gifts of psychological analysis and of sensitive feeling for the almost impalpable moral filaments that relate human beings to one another, the " surprizing Intimacy with the human Heart " lauded by Smollett. To him the *re*-action is all in all. It was this peculiar excellence of his friend's that Johnson had in the forefront of his mind when he likened Fielding's novels to the dial of a clock and Richardson to the visible works—not the happiest simile, from his point of view, since a clock exists for the purpose of telling the time of day and not for any opportunity it may afford us to " see wheels go round."

In a limited degree Richardson's psychological gift found scope in those brief flashes of self-betrayal which we are apt to call " dramatic," since they are the dramatist's almost sole resource. A perfect specimen of this is found in the last volume but one of *Grandison*. In a short sentence it reveals all the bane of uncertainty that Harriet Byron felt about the nature of her beloved Sir Charles's emotional relations with her rival, all her self-condemned jealousy, all her unladylike triumph (though, characteristically of her cruel position, it is, as she realizes, but a semi-triumph). Grandison has arranged an impromptu dance and Harriet has stood up for a minuet with him. She gives an account of the affair and the end of it runs : " I wonder if Lady Clementina ever danced with him."

As a general rule, however, the effectiveness of Richardson's " psychology " rests not on succinctness, but on prolixity. The workings of a mind stand revealed not in a sudden, uncommon moment of excitement, but through a series of outpourings when the pressure of events and blood is more normal.

For this procedure, clearly, the comparatively formless epistolary method afforded the greatest advantages, particularly where the personages under scrutiny owned a passion for letter-writing. A certain output *per* given space of time they felt it obligatory upon them to produce. They wrote, therefore, whether there was "anything to write about " or not and, again, they never entered on such a state of mental instability as would render them unfit to sit down to their writing-tables. In other words, they revealed themselves just as, with quite negligible exceptions, actual people reveal their natures to us in real life. The pace at which motive was disclosed and the constituent parts of an emotional complex laid bare was,

127

in general, infinitesimal : the observer could appreciate them at his leisure and become familiar with a slowly changing emotional situation exactly as if one of his own daily acquaintances were concerned.

The diffusiveness of Richardson's general method is particularly blatant, as it is peculiarly appropriate and useful, in those cases of divided mind, in the description and diagnosis of which Richardson is unexcelled ; and all Richardson's major psychological studies, it may be remarked again, concern the divided mind.

Clarissa affords the simplest example. In her we have at issue, during the most vital part of her biography, an undeniable affection for Lovelace with an admiration for certain of his qualities, notably those which Clarissa finds lacking in herself—energy and concentration upon the active execution of purpose ; these forces stand ranged on the one side ; on the other, her pride (" By my soul, Jack, she is a true daughter of the Harlowes ! "), which views her affection and admiration with disdain, prohibits her from forcing Lovelace's hand in both their interests (as she could have done) and from taking any step in a situation when it was clearly, according to the accepted code, Lovelace's duty to take all the steps, and then that innate decency bred of generations of honest living which, in similar circumstances, served Sophia Baines so much better. Later in Clarissa's story, the sense of utter outrage to her humanity is confronted with the recollection of her primal affection for her seducer (and is not an unresentful recollection of love a kind of affection still ?), with a completely assimilated Christian theory of forgiveness and a truly philosophical appreciation of the nullity of all earthly aspirations, ambitions and glories in the face of death. Similarly, in the earliest part of the book, Clarissa's motives derive their energy from the friction between those sentiments of decency and Christian piety already indicated and her resentment at the humiliating distrust on the part of those nearest to her for what she must have known to be her best qualities.

In Pamela, the pious opportunist, the mingling of motives is much more intricate because self-deception, partly clear to the author and partly hidden from him, was superadded. Pamela's ego, with everything against her, had a terrible game to play, whether we consider that game to be keeping " pure " or winning a great position. Not only was she handicapped by weakness and ignorance, but also on the former interpretation, by her own sensual nature (*videlicet* love for Mr. B——) and, on the second, by the hideous temptation to make sure of the second prize (Mr. B——'s very handsome terms of concubinage) at the risk of throwing away her chief chance of infinitely greater gain.

Harriet Byron, at first sight, does not seem to afford such an example of internal warfare. But further reflection—on, for instance, the sentence about the minuet with Sir Charles just quoted—will show that such a warfare existed, far, far down, barely discernible to Harriet herself, though quite clear, I think, to her creator : the debate, so familiar in more modern literature, between what one might call the primitive woman in her, wanting what she wants, especially if it be her elected mate, with a ferocity to which only Balzac has done justice, and a ladylike code, by no means uncongenial to her at most junctures of her life. The strife is made all the more painful, because of the conditions in which it takes place, with Harriet as the deeply obliged, admiring guest of the man she loves, unable to descry her fate, unable to stir a finger *pour corriger la fortune* and compelled from every consideration to keep polite, resigned and cheerful through it all—the " dead point " emotional situation, so incredibly difficult to realize in literature and so consummately indicated by Richardson. What havoc a similar contest between Mother Eve and repressive civilisation could work in a less self-controlled nature is seen, of course, in the deplorable parallel case of Charlotte Grandison, on whom the pressure of circumstance really weighed much less heavily than on Harriet.

A similar clash of motives clearly exists in the minds both of Lovelace and Sir Charles Grandison. Its nature, in the former instance, appeared in the short synopsis of *Clarissa* it was necessary to give. Striking, if hardly out of the way, it does not seem to have occupied Richardson's mind greatly and his analysis of it is much more summary, much more rough and ready, than that applied to Clarissa or Pamela. The working of a man's mind obviously did not much interest Richardson, while that of a woman's fascinated him. To this fact some of the ill success of *Grandison* must be attributed. The all-important dilemma in which Sir Charles finds himself at the heart of the story seems almost entirely physical. He is a piece of iron played upon by two different magnets. We are not made aware of any conflicting impulses within him urging him now to Clementina, now to Harriet. If Clementina's passion had only been a shade less decorous and kindled just a spark of something in Grandison which he would not have liked to have mentioned—say, reck-lessness—the book might have lost some of its insipidity ; but then Sir Charles would, according to the code, have lost his *raison d'être*, his impeccability.

As an example of Richardson's usual method of characterization and analysis of motive, one may take the turning-point in Pamela's emotional history, when she confesses aloud her love for Mr. B—— and reveals the real gravity of the struggle raging within her. (It must be borne in mind that a necessarily summarized account greatly detracts from the effectiveness of the illustration).

As soon as she has obtained a moment's breathing-space in the welter of uncertainty into which, with his alternate bullying and coaxing, Mr. B——has designedly thrown his intended prey, she and Mrs. Jewkes " heard, that he had like to have been drowned in crossing the stream, a few days ago, in pursuing his game." At once, in the next sentence, comes the reflection : " What is the matter, that with all his ill usage of me, I cannot hate him ? " She can find no immediate solution to the poser she has set herself, and the story temporarily moves away from the emotional field to that of action.

Mr. B—— now offers his famous " Articles," by which Pamela shall become " mistress of my person and fortune, as much as if the foolish ceremony had passed " ; and, finding himself vanquished in the ensuing debates, attempts the combination of fraud and force which *The Virgin in Eden* found so particularly distasteful. One would imagine that such treatment would turn the heroine's professedly neutral feelings into hatred, or, at the least, would restore that state of internal commotion from which she had just emerged. But no ; as soon as the hysterical spasms following on Mr. B——'s attempted rape have spent themselves, that state of calm returns. Mr. B—— takes Pamela for a walk in the garden, and she rebukes him for his recent conduct to her. But when Mr. B—— loses his temper at the freedom with which her " licentious tongue " lashes his " little puny freedoms " and bids her be off, she goes down on her knees to beg his forgiveness. Later in the day, Mr. B——, mollified, again fetches Pamela for a walk, by the pond.

" And it was by the side of this pond . . . that my present hopes, if I am not to be deceived again, began to dawn : which I presume to flatter myself with being a happy omen for me, as if God Almighty would show your poor sinful daughter how well I did to put my affiance in His goodness, and not to throw away myself, because my ruin seemed inevitable, to my short-sighted apprehension." [A marvellous sentence !]

She coquets with her lover and finds that he responds " with an ardour that was never before so agreeable to me." The state of her mind immediately below that of expressional consciousness has thus arrived at a right diagnosis of " what is the matter " with her. Then, on the material plane at least, the storm breaks out again. Recoiling before the abyss of his folly and asserting himself for the last time, Mr. B—— orders " his travelling chariot to be got ready with all speed," and bundles his bewitcher into it.

" I think," she comments demurely, " I was loath to leave the house. Can you believe it ?—What could be the matter with me, I wonder ?—I felt something so strange, and my heart was so lumpish !—I wonder what ailed me !—But this was so *unexpected* !—I believe that was all !—Yet I am very strange still. Surely, surely, I cannot be like the old murmuring Israelites, to long after the onions and garlic of Egypt, when they had suffered there such heavy bondage ? "

This self-deception hardly outlasts the writing down. "So away drove the chariot!" Pamela learns that a fellow-servant, Robin, has a letter for her, which she is to have next day. She wheedles it out of him " on great promises of secrecy, and making no use of it. I will try if I can open it without breaking the seal, and will take a copy of it by and by." She does so and learns that Mr. B—— " was just upon resolving to defy all the censures of the world, and to make you my wife." One great secret deserves another.

" Oh my dear parents, forgive me ! but I found, to my grief, before, that my heart was too partial in his favour ; but *now* with so much openness, so much affection; nay, so much *honour* too (which was all I had before doubted, and kept me on the reserve), I am quite over-come. This was a happiness, however, I had no reason to expect. But, to be sure, I must own to you, that I shall never be able to think of anybody in the world but him.—Presumption ! you will say ; and so it is : But love is not a voluntary thing : *Love*, did I say ?—But come, I hope not :—At least it is not, I hope, gone so far as to make me *very* uneasy : For I know not *how* it came, nor *when* it began ; but crept, crept it has, like a thief, upon me ; and before I knew what was the matter, it looked like love."

At this point, to clinch matters, she learns that Mr. B—— has fallen ill. She orders the chariot back at once. " . . . indeed, I longed to see him," she confesses without fur-ther ado.

The last longer passage quoted shows Richardson at his best : the triumphant emotion still clouded by its

133

adversary and betraying the narrowness of its victory by specious deprecations and the like ; and the whole cunningly built up, for all its simplicity of vocabulary, to culminate in the repetition of the all-important word. It may, indeed, be urged that the craftsmanship is too perfect, that Richardson's realism oversteps the bounds of probability. That Pamela should *think* in the way that Richardson represents her as thinking need not be doubted; but that she should, even with the most remarkable power of self-expression, ever *write* as she is supposed to is incredible. Writing is a mechanical art, in which the brain always outruns the hand ; and Pamela's intellect would have realized the implication of the fatal word "love" long before her pen set it down, and, in the circumstances, would have dictated something else.

§ 12

The account of Clarissa's death quoted earlier in this chapter as an illustration of Richardson's powers of pathos might also be cited here in exemplification of a second quality which has been hailed as supreme in him, though not as unanimously as his psychological insight. That quality is his skill in minute *genre*-painting, or, in a word, his Realism. The realistic method which he employed— and deliberately employed—appears both in that passage from *Clarissa* and in the one from *Grandison*, in which the heroine's sister was formally described. It consists of an accumulation of small facts or small traits, to all of which the same importance attaches and none of which can fairly be described as consummate. As a further specimen of it, applied to yet another class of subject, one

may adduce a passage from the introduction of the new
Lady Grandison to her home :

" EVERYBODY admires the elegance of this drawing-
room. The finest japan china that I ever saw, except
that of Lady G——'s which she so whimsically received
at the hands of her lord, took particularly every female
eye.

Sir Charles led me into a closet adjoining—Your
oratory, your library, my love, when you shall have furnished it, as you desired you might, by your chosen collection from Northamptonshire.

It is a sweet little apartment : elegant book-cases,
unfurnished. Every other ornament complete. How
had he been at work to oblige me, by Dr. Bartlett's good
offices, while my heart, perhaps, was torn, part of the
time, with uncertainty !

The housekeeper, a middle-aged woman, who is
noted, as you have heard her master say, for prudence,
integrity, and obligingness, a gentlewoman born, appearing,
Sir Charles presented her to me. Receive, my love, a
faithful, a discreet gentlewoman, who will think herself
honoured with your commands. Mrs. Curzon (to her),
you will be happy in a mistress who is equally beloved
and reverenced by all who have the honour of her countenance, if she approve of your services, and if you choose
to continue with us.

I took her hand : I hope, Mrs. Curzon, there is no
doubt but you will. You may depend upon everything
that is in my power to make you happy.

She looked pleased ; but answered only with a respectful
courtesy.

Sir Charles led the gentlemen out to show them his

study. We just looked into a fine suite of rooms on the same floor, and joined there.

We found my uncle and Mr. Deane admiring the disposition of everything, as well as the furniture. The glass cases are neat, and, as Dr. Bartlett told us, stored with well-chosen books in all sciences. Mr. Deane praised the globes, the orrery, and the instruments of all sorts, for geographical, astronomical, and other scientifical observations. It is ornamented with pictures, some, as Dr. Bartlett told us, of the best masters of the Italian and Flemish schools ; statues, bustoes, bronzes : and there also, placed in a distinguished manner, were the two rich cabinets of medals, gems, and other curiosities, presented to him by Lady Olivia. He mentioned what they contained, and by whom presented ; and said he would show us at leisure the contents. They are not mine, added he. I only give them a place till the generous owner shall make some worthy man happy. *His* they must be. It would be a kind of robbery to take them from a family, that, for near a century past, have been collecting them."

In this passage Richardson intended primarily to draw a picture, in which animate and inanimate objects stand on very much the same footing ; and the result is perfectly satisfactory. But when the same method is applied to the living subject and it is required to show the lifelikeness and liveliness of that subject, it tends in effect, as was noted of the portraiture of Miss Grandison, to appear a little flat, insipid and, when unrelieved, monotonous. Richardson was at pains to supply relief by various means ; asides and longer comments, dialogue to interlard description, generalizations and inserted anecdotes. He also essayed a lighter general tenor, of which one specimen,

from a sub-plot, has been given and of which another may
here be added : the visit of one of Miss Byron's suitors in
the company of his match-making uncle :

" Miss Byron to Miss Selby.
Monday Night—Tuesday Morning, February 6-7.

SIR ROWLAND and his nephew, tea being not quite
ready, sat down with my cousins ; and the knight, leaving
Mr. Fowler little to say, expatiated so handsomely on his
nephew's good qualities, and great passion for me, and on
what he himself proposed to do for him in addition to his
own fortune, that my cousins, knowing I liked not the
gentlemen in our neighbourhood, and thought very
indifferently of Sir Hargrave, were more than half inclined
to promote the addresses of Mr. Fowler ; and gave them
both room to think so.

This favourable disposition set the two gentlemen up.
They were impatient for tea, that they might see me.

By the time I had sealed up my letters, word was
brought me that tea was ready ; and I went down.

The knight, it seems, as soon as they heard me coming,
jogged Mr. Fowler.—Nephew, said he, pointing to the
door, see what you can say to the primrose of your heart !
This is now the primrose season with us in Caermarthen,
Mr. Reeves.

Mr. Fowler, by a stretch of complaisance, came to
meet and introduce me to the company, though at home.
The knight nodded his head after him, smiling ; as if he
had said, let my nephew alone to gallant the lady to her
seat.

I was a little surprised at Mr. Fowler's approaching me
the moment I appeared, and with his taking my hand,

and conducting me to my seat, with an air ; not knowing how much he had been raised by the conversation that had passed before.

He bowed. I courtesied, and looked a little sillier than ordinary, I believe.

Your servant, young lady, said the knight. Lovelier, and lovelier, by mercy ! How these blushes become that sweet face !—But, forgive me, madam, it is not my intent to dash you.

Writing, Miss Byron, all day ! said Mrs. Reeves. We have greatly missed you.

My cousin seemed to say this, on purpose to give me time to recover myself.

I have blotted several sheets of paper, said I, and had just concluded.

I hope, madam, said the knight, leaning forward his whole body, and peering in my face under his bent brows, that *we* have not been the cause of hastening you down.

I stared. But as he seemed not to mean anything, I would not help him to a meaning by my own over-quickness.

Mr. Fowler had done an extraordinary thing, and sat down, hemmed, and said nothing : looking, however, as if he was at a loss to know whether he or his uncle was expected to speak.

The cold weather was then the subject ; and the two gentlemen rubbed their hands, and drew nearer the fire, as if they were the colder for talking of it. Many hems passed between them, now the uncle looking on the nephew, now the nephew on the uncle : at last they fell into talk of their new-built house at Caermarthen, and the furnishing of it.

They mentioned afterwards their genteel neighbourhood, and gave the characters of half a dozen people, of whom none present but themselves ever heard ; but all tending to shew how much they were valued by the best gentry in Caermarthenshire.

The knight then related a conversation that had once passed between himself and the late Lord Mansell, in which that nobleman had complimented him on an estate of a clear £3,000 a year, besides a good deal of ready cash, and with supposing that he would set up his nephew, when of age (for it was some years ago), as a representative for the county. And he repeated the *prudent* answer he gave his lordship, disavowing such a design, as no better than a gaming *propensity*, as he called it, which had ruined many a fair estate.

This sort of talk, in which his nephew *could* bear a part (and indeed they had it all between them), held the tea-time ; and then having given themselves the consequence they seemed to intend, the knight, drawing his chair nearer to me, and winking to his nephew, who withdrew, began to set forth to me the young gentleman's good qualities ; to declare the passion he had for me ; and to beg my encouragement of so worthy, so *proper*, and so *well-favoured* a young man : who was to be his sole heir ; and for whom he would do such things, on my account, as, during his life, he would not do for any other woman *breathing*.

There was no answering a discourse so serious, with the air of levity which it was hardly possible to avoid assuming on the first visit of the knight.

I was vexed that I found myself almost as bashful, as silly, and as silent, as if I had thoughts of encouraging Mr. Fowler's addresses. My cousins seemed pleased with my bashfulness. The knight, I once thought, by the tone of his voice, and his hum, would have struck up a Welsh tune, and dance for joy.

Shall I call in my kinsman, madam, to confirm all I have said, and to pour out his whole soul at your feet ? My boy is bashful : but a little favour from that sweet countenance will make a man of him.   Let me, let me, call in my boy.   I will go for him myself ; and was going.

Let me say one word, Sir Rowland—before Mr. Fowler comes in—before you speak to him—you have explained yourself unexceptionably.   I am obliged to you and Mr. Fowler for your good opinion : but this can never be."

§ 13

Nothing that we know about our author suggests that he had a genuine sense of humour.   So, like all humourless men who aim at the comic (Victor Hugo is the great literary example), his most resolute efforts in that direction usually landed him, at his most fortunate, into the grotesque.   Not infrequently this is perfectly appropriate. The exaggerated ugliness of Mrs. Jewkes, for example, who "is as thick as she is long," and the melodramatic ferocity of M. Colbrand, Mr. B——'s Swiss servant, figures of anti-mask, are excused by Pamela's fears. The mulish gloom of the senior Harlowes might produce an effect akin to the farcical in certain circumstances or if unduly stressed ; but the author carefully keeps it within proper bounds, so that we are prepared even to credit the report Colonel Morden makes on them when they hear the provisions of Clarissa's will :

"The clothes, the thirty guineas for mourning to

Mrs. Norton, with the recommendation of the good woman for housekeeper at The Grove, were thought sufficient, had the article of £600, which was called monstrous, been omitted. Some other passages in the will were called *flights, and such whimsies as distinguish people of imagination from those of judgment.*"

But even here, as in the scenes where Anna Howe or Charlotte Grandison take the centre of the stage, a sober eye will see how uncertain Richardson's propensity towards humorous or quasi-humorous exaggeration could make his hold on reality. Comic painting (in Fielding's comparison) was always tending to lapse into caricatura, exactly as in Smollett. To prove this point—which accounts in part for the disparagement of his perfectly genuine, if inconstant powers as a realist—one need only study one of Richardson's great set descriptions, his account of the dying bawd Sinclair, and observe how it begins with a sobriety and ruthless veracity unsurpassed by any other writer and finally, when the note is forced, turns to something very near burlesque.

" There were no less than eight of her cursed daughters surrounding her bed when I entered ; one of her partners Polly Horton, at their head ; and now Sally, her other partner, and *Madam* Carter, as they called her (for they are all *Madams* with one another), made the number ten : all in shocking deshabille, and without stays, except Sally, Carter, and Polly ; who, not daring to leave her, had not been in bed all night. The other seven seemed to have been but just up, risen perhaps from their customers in the fore-house, and their nocturnal orgies, with faces, three or four of them, that had run, the paint lying in streaky seams not half blowzed off, discovering coarse wrinkled skins : the hair of some of them of divers colours, obliged to the black-lead comb where black was affected ; the artificial jet, however, yielding apace to the natural brindle ; that of others plastered with oil and powder ; the oil predominating : but every one's hanging about her ears and neck in broken curls, or ragged ends ; and each at my entrance taken with one motion, stroking their matted locks with both hands under their coifs, mobs or pinners, every one of which was awry. They were all slip-shoed ; stockingless some ; only under-petticoated all; their gowns, made to cover straddling hoops, hanging trollopy, and tangling about their heels ; but hastily wrapt round them, as soon as I came up stairs. And half of them (unpadded, shoulder-bent, pallid-lipt, limber-jointed wretches) appearing from a blooming nineteen or twenty perhaps over-night, haggard well-worn strumpets of thirty-eight or forty.

I am the more particular in describing to thee the appearance these creatures made in my eyes when I came into the room, because I believe thou never sawest any of them, much less a group of them, thus unprepared for being seen.[1] I, for my part, never did before ; nor had I now, but upon this occasion, being thus *favoured*. If thou *hadst*, I believe thou wouldst hate a profligate woman, as one of Swift's yahoos, or Virgil's obscene harpies, squirting their ordure upon the Trojan trenches ; since the persons of such in their retirements are as filthy

---

[1] Whoever has seen Dean Swift's Lady's Dressing-room, will think this description of Mr. Belford's not only more *natural*, but more *decent painting*, as well as better justified by the design, and by the *use* that may be made of it. [Richardson's own footnote : Mr. Belford, of course, is the supposed reporter of this scene.]

as their minds.—Hate them as much as I do ; and as much as I admire, and next to adore, a truly virtuous and elegant woman : for to me it is evident, that as a neat and clean woman must be an angel of a creature, so a sluttish one is the impurest animal in nature. But these were the veterans, the chosen band ; for now and then flitted in to the number of half a dozen more, by turns, subordinate sinners, under-graduates, younger than some of the chosen phalanx, but not less obscene in their appearance, though indeed not so much beholden to the plastering fucus ; yet unpropt by stays, squalid, loose in attire, sluggish-haired, under-petticoated only as the former, eyes half-opened, winking and pinking, mispatched, yawning, stretching, as if from the unworn-off effects of the midnight revel ; all armed in succession with supplies of cordials (of which every one present was either taster or partaker) under the direction of the busier Dorcas, who frequently popped in, to see her slops duly given and taken. But when I approached the *old wretch*, what a spectacle presented itself to my eyes !

Her misfortune has not at all sunk, but rather, as I thought, increased her flesh ; rage and violence perhaps swelling her muscular features. Behold her, then, spreading the whole troubled with her huge quaggy car-cass ; her broad hands clenched with violence ; her big eyes, goggling and flaming red we may suppose those of a salamander ; her matted grisly hair, made irreverent (*sic !*) by her wickedness (her clouted head-dress being half off, spread about her fat ears and brawny neck) ; her livid lips parched, and working violently ; her broad chin in convulsive motion ; her wide mouth, by reason of the contraction of her forehead (which seemed to be half lost in its own frightful furrows) splitting her face, as it

were, in two parts ; and her huge tongue hideously rolling
in it ; heaving, puffing as if for breath ; her bellows-
shaped and various coloured breasts ascending by turns to
her chin, and descending out of sight, with the violence of
her gaspings."

§ 14

The dissentients from the praise due to Richardson's
realism were not all moved by artistic considerations ; the
majority among them, no doubt, detested and denied his
realism, as all realism is decried at every new advance,
because it revealed things about themselves or mankind in
general which they hated to acknowledge as true. Yet
others, though personally and emotionally unaffected by
the findings of the realistic method, questioned its accuracy
and a sufficient knowledge of the materials on which it
ostensibly worked. In so doing, of course, they raised a
doubt, which it is important to canvass, of Richardson's
reliability as a social historian of his time.

One of them, fortunately, Lady Mary Wortley Montagu, expressed herself rather fully on this topic—though,
in assessing the value of her criticism, we must bear in
mind that when she made her observations she had been
living abroad for many years and that her somewhat
eccentric nature had debarred her from the society and
environment of perfectly average people for even longer.
After reading *Clarissa* for at least the second time and
confirming her first impression, she writes to her daughter:

" This Richardson is a strange fellow. I heartily
despise him, and eagerly read him, nay, sob over his
works in a most scandalous manner. The two first

tomes of Clarissa touched me, as being very resembling to
my maiden days ; and I find in the pictures of Sir Thomas
Grandison and his lady, what I have heard of my mother,
and seen of my father."

The concession made in this passage is very valuable ; for
in his first works Richardson deliberately set the story
somewhat back in time, and the rather old-fashioned
atmosphere Lady Mary apprehended was, therefore, no
blunder of his, but something consciously evoked. A
month later Lady Mary has been reading *Grandison*, for
the first time, and begins her report :

" I have now read over Richardson—he sinks hor-
ribly in his third volume (he does so in his story of Clarissa).
When he talks of Italy, it is plain he is no better acquainted
with it than he is with the kingdom of Mancomugi.
[Then follows a long elaboration of this, coupled with
denunciations of the Roman faith and some sane observations on the Romantic fallacies of insanity ; she goes on]
Richardson is as ignorant in morality as he is in anatomy
. . . and I believe this author was never admitted into
higher company, and should confine his pen to the amours
of housemaids, and the conversation at the steward's
table, where I imagine he has sometimes intruded, though
oftener in the servants' hall. . . .
Richardson never had probably money enough to
purchase . . . even a ticket for a masquerade, which
gives him such an aversion to them ; though his intended
satire against them is very absurd on the account of his
Harriet, since she might have been carried off in the same
manner if she had been going from supper with her grand-
mamma. . . . He has no idea of the manners of high

life : his old Lord M. talks in the style of a country justice, and his virtuous young ladies romp like the wenches round a maypole."

By a lucky chance positive evidence from an unexpected source assures us that one of Lady Mary's shafts hit the mark right in the centre. Richardson *did* write, with no abatement of his realistic style, about things with which he had no first-hand acquaintanceship—and actually prided himself on such a lapse ! In terms almost identical with those that he had employed nearly three years earlier in discussing the same matter with the elder Mrs. Chapone he wrote to his Dutch translator, Stinstra : " I never, to my knowledge, was in a vile House, or in Company with a lewd Woman, in my Life. So have I, in Pamela described, with Approbation, a Masquerade Scene, yet never was present at one."

Richardson, then, knew nothing at first hand about "fast life," and we may readily believe Lady Mary's further censure that Italy and its ways were completely *terra incognita* to him. What about the third charge, that he had " No idea of the manners of high life ? " Here, too, Lady Mary seems justified. Chesterfield, otherwise much more favourably disposed to the author of *Clarissa* than she, complained that " Whenever he goes *Ultra crepidam*, into high life, he grossly mistakes the modes." On consideration indeed we find that socially the most eminent of Richardson's friends, Lady Bradshaigh and her sister, Young, the Duchess of Portland's intimate, Mark Hildesley, Bishop of Sodor and Man and a descendant of Edward III, hardly attained the level of the Harlowes and Grandisons. Possible, but slight exceptions are afforded by Secker, the *bourgeois* Archbishop of Canterbury who, according to Horace Walpole, ran a race with Sherlock for the old ladies and, more obviously, by the Speaker, the Right Honourable Arthur Onslow. Of him Richardson makes a good deal of play in correspondence, notably with their common friend Edwards, but we have little positive assurance of intimacy. As far as mere *manners* go, accordingly, Richardson cannot be looked on as an entirely reliable social historian : *Pamela*, it would seem, approximates most closely to a transcript from reality—*Pamela*, which describes " from below " the life of Midland squires in 1720 or thereabout, quarter of a century before Richardson wrote of it. But his realism covered much ground beside manners— "*tous les détails domestiques* " which Madame du Deffand found so enchanting and which were so entirely novel in literature. Of the *milieu*, the material background to the lives of the comfortable classes, Richardson gives us a more complete and veracious account than any conscious *littérateur* before 1800.

§ 15

In concluding this discussion of Richardson's art, we came to a consideration of a last elusive abstraction, the subject's style. The most diverse opinions have been expressed about it. Lord Chesterfield writes to Madame du Boccage about *Clarissa* : " Celui qui l'a écrite, qui est aussi l'autheur de *Pamela*, est un Libraire, qui manque du savoir et de style ; " another master of the artfully simple, Robert Louis Stevenson, declares on the other hand of that same work that Richardson wrote with " the pen of an angel," a dictum that recalls another midway in time between the two, uttered by the Reverend Percivale Stockdale (who could never, he said, forget how

SAMUEL RICHARDSON

Clarissa engaged and enraptured his fancy, how it excited and influenced the moral emotions of his heart). " I should warmly recommend," he continues, " the novels of RICHARDSON, in preference to any book of mere human theology." Young people "would hear the simple and pathetick oratory of CHRIST, without the formality, and glow, and false terrours of the priest."

In general, however, Richardson's pathetick oratory receives less notice and commendation than the raciness of his language, which, in spite of the rising social level, is more in evidence in his later than in his early work, when he was still finding his feet and haunted by the exemplary influence of the *Familiar Letters*. Successive commentators have remarked that his lack of conventionality in expression greatly shocked his translators, and this in spite of the fact that he was one of the cleanest-mouthed writers of his age and certainly in this respect by far the " purest " among the major novelists up to the time of Scott.

In the more narrowly technical department information is not easy to obtain. Dr. Uhrström's admirable treatise, *Studies in the Language of Samuel Richardson* (Upsala 1907), approaches the subject from the standpoint of the twentieth century, demonstrating the particulars in which Richardson's language seems strange, from obsolescence or otherwise, to us of the twentieth century. One would welcome a companion study showing wherein he was an innovator. In the absence of any expert philological opinion, one may conjecture that Richardson introduced from colloquial, and perhaps even dialectal, sources a number of words and phrases into the language of literature, or at the least lent his immense prestige to many already introduced from popular comedy and operetta, the memoirs of rogues etcetera, but fighting hard for recognition. At all events, that is what contemporaries of a philological bent criticized, unfavourably for the most part, in his writings : words like *froppishness* and *lumpish* had probably come in before " Richard Conqueror," but it was a shock to meet them in a drawing-room or library.

Richardson certainly cannot be set up as a stylistic revolutionary—he is too clumsy, as the historian of English prose rhythm has declared. His characters " of a certain rank in life " always come back, in spite of occasional vagaries, to the legacy of *The Spectator* as their norm, but the realistic aim to which he was fairly true compelled him to put less high-flown or polished and more colloquial language into the mouths and pens of his humbler characters. Sometimes, indeed, they are made to use the wholly irregular ungrammatical and unorthographical language condemned (and used) by the educated ; in general, however, they arrive—as always happens in literature—at a compromise between the King's and their own English, which may pass muster as " literature." In this small way, as so often, Richardson, for all his conservative caution and the precedents he could allege, foreshadows revolution—that break-up of the " classical style " begun with the " Romantic Revival " and carried to its present limit (in prose literature) by Mr. James Joyce.

Chapter Five

SENTIMENT AND THE AGE

§ 1

Like all other ages in this changing world, the age in which Richardson lived was, in every respect, an age of transition. This is most plainly evident in the realm of thought, in which the new conceptions of man and the universe formulated by Locke and Newton were slowly and arduously ousting the old orthodoxy. Unhappily Richardson and Philosophy lie so far apart, that the latter cannot be properly used as a base for estimating the former's position in the firmament of his age. The wide, flat expanse of politics affords a better starting-place for such a survey.

Beneath the prosperous placidity of the year following on the Treaties of Utrecht, political changes of great consequences were preparing and taking shape. They were symbolized, towards the end of Richardson's life, by the calling to power of Pitt the elder and by the sobriquet he bore of "the great Commoner." To the great nobles who shared the government of England in the days of William and Anne had succeeded the country gentleman Walpole and, after fifteen years of political instability, he was followed by the nominee and champion of mercantile interests. Aforetime, the greatness of a country

150

had been gauged by the splendour of its court or the magnitude of its standing army : De Foe taught the world to read it in the price of funds on the London Stock Exchange. This philistine doctrine of his did not gain universal assent for many decades to come, the reign of a middle-class which virtually absorbed the aristocracy was not complete or unchallenged at any point in the eighteenth century. But many characteristics of such a reign, which were to develop to perfection a hundred years after De Foe's death and be epitomized in the party-cry of " Peace, Retrenchment, and Reform," can already be discerned. Walpole leads the company of great financial prime-ministers whose energies are bent towards obtaining cheap money for king and subject and making administration as economical as circumstances allow. For over twenty years he managed to keep his country and most of the rest of the world at peace. Even state-abetted reform makes a shy appearance in his time. The satirists, so plentiful and popular in societies which do nothing to remedy the abuses pilloried by them, become less frequent, and the practical reformers (soon to be called Utilitarians), with finished schemes for new or reformed institutions in their pockets, inherit their place and access to the public ear. The Highways Act of 1741, which inaugurated the era of speedy and ever accelerating transport, together with government road-making in the north a few years later, is one sign of the times ; another the overdue reorganization of the metropolitan police-system, in which Henry Fielding played so gallant a part ; a third the inauguration of large charitable foundations on all but a national scale, like the Foundling Hospital in 1739 and, nineteen years later, the Magdalen Hospital in which Richardson himself took great interest.

SAMUEL RICHARDSON

§ 2

Literature shows a similar drift. The puritan middle class whose wealth and energy were gaining political supremacy for it could also use that wealth to endow and that energy to produce literature of which it approved ; indeed, in displacing the single patron in favour of a body of subscribers, it introduced into literature, as Leslie Stephen acutely pointed out, that same joint-stock system which insured its financial and political strength.

The artistic ideals current in the early years of the eighteenth century, the "classicism" beloved of the courtiers and the aristocrats and the men of letters whom they admitted to their company, were constantly attacked and modified by writers standing outside that small circle and not impatient to enter it. De Foe and, more particularly, Addison and Steele laboured to establish a compromise in literary as well as ethical ideals, corresponding to the mixture of classes in the coffee-houses ; and their activities certainly resulted in that peculiarly English type of classicism—puritan, moral and catholic, as compared with its continental counterparts—which found, quite late, its supreme embodiment in Samuel Johnson. But their compromise did not for some time win very widespread acceptance, except perhaps in the realm of behaviour. The most interesting literature immediately after their time is, for the most part, written by unconverted classics of the older order, like Prior, Gay, Swift and Pope, or else by writers for whose taste Steele and his like had evidently not pioneered far enough in the dark forest of unorthodoxy.

The drama affords perhaps the best illustration of the

general development of literature in the first decades of the eighteenth century. The onslaught of Jeremy Collier on the Profaneness and Immorality of the English Stage in 1698 could not but find favour with a large section of middle-class opinion—not merely with that ultra-puritan wing of it which bestowed equal applause on Law's *Absolute Unlawfulness of the Stage Entertainment* twenty-eight years later, but also with the more liberally minded, who resented the usual picture which contemporary comedy gave of them as grotesque usurers, swindling lawyers, toyshop-keepers, cuckolds and wantons, existing mainly in order to supply the excesses of frivolous men about town.

In endeavouring to reconcile the demands on the one hand of the aristocratic exquisites to whom Congreve and Vanburgh generally addressed themselves (*i.e.*, the demand for an amusing evening's entertainment) and, on the other, of the middle-classes in whose midst the impoverished theatres could divine a great potential public (*i.e.*, the demand for edification and public decency) Steele, as we might expect, took the lead. Though that half of *The Tender Husband* (1705) which justified the title of the play clearly derives from the most notorious of Restoration comedies, Wycherley's *Country Wife*, it can offend the sense of decorum in no one content to enjoy its superficial meaning. The hard wit of Congreve is replaced by a captivating good humour and humanity ; and the final *éclaircissement* between husband and wife does not take the form of epigrammatic syllogisms concluded in a reconcilement whose basis may turn out little more substantial than a quibble : instead, either party is dissolved in tears, promising in a paroxysm of repentance to leave off the rather trivial delinquencies that have precipitated the

153

scene. To be sure, the improvements made on the current type of comedy could not content a strict critic quarter of a century afterwards, like Pamela ; the City, too, still appears in an unfavourable light, since its denizens are represented by a damsel crazed with romance-reading, a marriage-broker, a rich niggard and an amorous old maid. This blemish, however, Steele carefully removed in *The Conscious Lovers* (1722), in which the social and ethical accomplishments of the merchant Sealand and his two daughters fall not a whit below those of polished Sir John Bevil and his son.

The compromise attempted by Steele, though supported once more by Addison (in *The Drummer*, 1716) and no less a stage-personality than Colley Cibber, whose comedy of *Love's Last Shift* (1696) had anticipated Steele's in many ways, did not maintain itself in his time. Its failure may, indeed, be laid to the charge of the same Colley Cibber, in whom the moralizing strain was invariably overwhelmed by the scenes of frivolity in which he excelled as an actor.

Instead, then, of some more or less " agreed " poetic, we observe a somewhat mitigated continuance of the old frivolous tradition in comedy (and of the heroic tradition in tragedy), soon confronted by a radically different body of drama, which was not only animated by new ideals, but minded altogether to oust its rival. The new species is the domestic drama, inspired by certain Elizabethan pieces, made illustrious by Lillo, favoured by Fielding during the time in which he was closely associated with the stage, and probably damaged more than any other type by the infamous Licensing Act of 1737—a definitely aristocratic measure, it may be noted, since it riveted on to the theatre more closely the slackened trammels of court tutelage (without contributing any of its advantages). In these plays, of which Lillo's *London Merchant, or the History of George Barnwell* (1731) may be taken as the type, the doctrinaire purpose is all in all, and the *bourgeoisie* is set in the forefront of the scene, with all its virtues of probity, hard work, sobriety and benevolence, which are shown as giving happiness and possessing "survival-value," while dishonesty, idleness, extravagance, dishonourable or "gallant" love and selfishness meet with execration and the punishment of extinction.

§ 3

The new forces, crude as they still might be, which were finding a literary outlet in the domestic drama, received a complete check when the Licensing Act authorized the Lord Chamberlain to decide how far they might go. As we know, Fielding, one of the most promising of the new playwrights, gave up the theatre ; and it is perhaps not too fanciful to suggest that the suppressed genius of English literature which drove him to the novel five years later may likewise have escaped through the ready pen of his traditional rival a few months earlier.

Before that time, prose fiction had stood somewhat aside from the main body of literature, exempt alike from its glories and vagaries. The reason for its relative isolation may be found in the circumstance that, for good and ill, it had never received formal recognition by the literary dictators of antiquity and subsequent framers of artistic "rules." Boileau, to be sure, had written on the *héros de roman*, but had not thought fit to publish his disquisition during his lifetime ; the learned bishop, Huet, had contributed a long history of the genus by way of introduction to Segrais and Madame de la Fayette's *Zayde* ; but there had never arisen any acrimonious debates or pontifical pronouncements about Episodes, Diction, the Place of the Supernatural, the Unities, such as Tragedy and the Epic called forth.

In spite of such neglect—perhaps because of it—the novel had flourished : had flourished even in France and Italy, the homes of literary criticism, but also in Spain and in England, where theory counted for so little in comparison with untutored practice. Two distinct categories appeared at the outset : the " idealistic " novel, which one may define as fiction representing life and human nature as the author would like them to be rather than as he knows them to be, and the " realistic " novel, for which the reverse is true. The latter type, first given importance in England by Thomas Nashe with *The Unfortunate Traveller, or, the Life of Jacke Wilton* (1594), had thenceforth become almost identified with the so-called " picaresque " novel, the tale of peripatetic and considered villainy. During Richardson's lifetime, however, it had been lifted out of that rut by Daniel De Foe, who, in most of his novels, interested himself and his public in the predicaments of average humanity or, at least, of criminal characters whose mode of life and moral code were shown as perversions due to circumstance and not to deliberate volition. De Foe did for the suspect realistic novel what Cibber and Steele had done for comedy : he moralized it, at any rate a good part, partly by interlarding it with unimpeachable maxims and reflections, partly by endeavouring to made it really fulfil the purpose insincerely avowed by his predecessors, that of reforming by means of deterrent example.

For us in this place the history of the other category, the "idealistic," possesses the greater relevance. It began, as far at least as English literature is concerned, as an off-shoot of the didactic book of manners. Castiglione's *Libro del Cortegiano*, Englished (1561) as *The Courtier* by Sir Thomas Hoby, may stand for the type, but two native products, Sir Thomas Elyot's *Governour* (1531) and Ascham's *Scholemaster* (1570), though not so representative, show how quick England was to follow a general European fashion. It was from the latter of these two works that virtually the oldest English novelist, John Lyly, derived the name for the eponymous hero of his first novel, *Euphues, the Anatomy of Wit* (1580), wherein, to quote the title, "are contained the delights that Wit [*i.e.*, Intellect] followeth in his youth, of the pleasauntnesse of loue : and the happinesse he reapeth in age by the perfectance of wisdom." The author of *Euphues* and his imitators were, indeed, less eager to relate an arbitrary series of events about imaginary characters than to instruct their readers how to think and act justly, as well as express themselves, in certain circumstances of life, notably those in which the sentiments were engaged—a predilection, as we have seen, precisely corresponding to Richardson's. Among the works directly and indirectly called forth by *Euphues*, two are worth noting here, *The Countess of Pembroke's Arcadia* (1590) by Sir Philip Sidney, in which the emotional springs of action are considered with some care, and Greene's *Pandosto* (1588), the source of Shakespeare's *Winter's Tale*.

Even when unconcerned with highway robbery, prose fiction during the seventeenth century looks, at first sight, further removed in everything but diction from that of the following century than does that of the sixteenth century. Ascham's accusation against the tales of Malory, that they comprise nothing but open manslaughter and bold bawdry, apparently fits it equally well. But closer study shows that the aim of Lyly and his kind, by pleasant means to effect a refinement of manners, is equally persistent in the minds of Mademoiselle de Scudéry and her kind, whether in France or England. Indeed, the notorious *Carte de Tendre*, drawn and described amidst the convolutions of her *Clélie* and about the only thing remembered of its ten volumes, affords a perfect example of this. It affords at the same time a perfect example of the novel's steady advance by a process of direct development. For in instructing the would-be Compleat Lover what he should shun and what seek, whither different modes of " attack " may lead him, it shows him diagrammatically in what relation the different amatory or sentimental emotions and their stimuli stand to one another : how he who skirts the craggy rocks of Pride, will find the villages Indiscretion, Perfidy, Slander and Malice successively harbouring him until he reaches the Sea of Enmity ; how, most significant of all, the goals of his wayfaring lie very, very near to *La Mer Dangereuse* and *Terres Inconnues* ;—and so forth. In other words, processes of mind and sentimental analysis were, however superficially, claiming in those heroic romances which Mrs. Pepys read, a share of the attention otherwise concentrated on deeds of valour, incredible virtues and mazy intrigue.

It is probably true that for two generations after Mademoiselle de Scudéry gave up novel-writing the average novelist possessed no profounder insight or interest in psychology or behaviour than she did. But the shrinkage in other attractions tended to throw these qualities into stronger relief. In Madame de La Fayette's *Princesse de Clèves* (1678) what the two men *do*, " how it all fits in " and " ends," are clearly things of little moment when contrasted with the mental and emotional processes of the three protagonists and with the ethical problem which they combine to raise. Madame de La Fayette, of course, was no average novelist ; but what, with extraordinary skill and economy, she succeeded in doing was by no means alien from the ambitions of her weaker sisters.

Of these there were many, not only in France, but also in this country, where the English *Princess of Cleves* appeared in 1688. Only one of the latter sort, however, survives in the text-books : and that is Mrs. Aphra Behn, who died in the same year that Richardson was born. But Mrs. Behn was succeeded in her craft by Mrs. Manley, Mrs. Aubin, Mrs. Davys, Mrs. Barker, Mrs. Haywood, only to mention some of the less obscure. All of these were writing when Richardson was a youngish man, and some of them continued to turn out their fictions until after the publication of *Grandison*. In their sensationalism and improbability and the strange names which the characters boast, these narratives were apt to resemble those comparatively short tales which Mademoiselle de Scudéry had used as " inset-stories " in her interminable romances. Such, for instance, is the anonymous *Clorana* of 1737, which deserves a special note for its full title (*The History of Clorana. The Beautiful Arcadian or Virtue Triumphant*) and for the fact that characters called Clarissa and Clementina occur in it. It deals with complicated love-affairs among the princes of fictitious countries. Usually, however, the characters have by this time descended somewhat in the social scale and the scene was, as a general rule, laid nearer home and less remote from the time of writing ; great stress was laid on the extravagant emotions under which, at suitable crises, the actors were alleged to labour and upon the fine sentiments which they then uttered :—all presented in the palpable endeavour to rouse as much admiration and, more especially, pity, as might be. Their failure effectively to do so was mainly due to their general incoherence: as the different parts of the story were badly articulated, so it was impossible for the reader to reconstruct whole, living and credible figures from the ill-sorted bundles of deeds, feelings and mouthings which the authors labelled with their names. Nevertheless, however poorly they may have realized it, the importance which the novelists attached to their endeavour of rousing emotion must not be underrated : nor must their belief that all emotions, and particularly the "gentler" emotions, possess an ethical value in themselves, irrespective of cause or effect, remain unnoticed.

§ 4

Both the realism and the emotionalism on which the rival schools of popular novelists a generation on either side of 1700 relied, received a strong impetus from a work whose outstanding peculiarity of form gives it a special interest to those concerned with Richardson and his art. That is the collection of *cris du cœur* published at Cologne in 1669 as *Lettres Portugaises*, in which a nun exclaimed against the faithlessness of her lover and, in doing so, betrayed the intensity of her own passion and some of the details of the romantic intrigue into which it had hurried her. It has since transpired that the five letters were written by an actual person in the actual circumstances described, by a canoness of Beja in Portugal called Mariana d'Alcoforado ; but the general, if not universally avowed view of them in the seventeenth and eighteenth century (when they were continually reprinted) regarded them as fictions, albeit of the most consummate realism. Imitations accordingly abounded. From this time on the " letter-novel " became a recognized sub-species. So, in England, we have (after the translation of the original *Lettres Portugaises* by Roger L'Estrange in 1678), the *Love Letters between a Nobleman and his Sister* (1693) and the *Letters Written by Mrs. Manley* (1696), which ingratiated themselves by the addition of " A Letter from a supposed Nun in *Portugal*, to a Gentleman in *France*, in Imitation of the Nun's Five Letters in Print, by Colonel *Pack*." Mrs. Manley used her epistolary device merely for giving a racy account of men and manners as observed on a Stage-Coach Journey between London and Exeter. The credit for first telling, by this means and in English, an invented tale, in which plot counts for as much as sentiments or description, belongs to the versatile Tom Brown of Shifnal, whose *Adventures of Lindamira*, later called *The Lover's Secretary*, appeared in 1702. The story in this novel, which is narrated in the first person singular, is divided up into twenty-four sections, but, instead of each section being called a chapter, it is made up, by the addition of a superscription and subscription, into a " Letter " from the heroine to her " Freind in the Country." The technique is no more complex or singular than that. It is, moreover, the technique which Marivaux, the first really important successor to Madame de la Fayette in the direct line, employed in his two major novels, *La Vie de Marianne* (1731-41) and *Le Paysan Parvenu.*

The letter has much in common with the journal ; when, indeed, a man or woman keeps a journal, not merely for the love of it, but with some idea that others may at a later time read it, it hardly differs at all from a correspondence in its content and its mixture of self-revelation and self-disguisement. But all journals, and especially those of whose fortunes the writers are careless, are to a greater or less extent " confessions," the purging of an individual soul. There is, therefore, generally an element of seriousness in journals, which is not a universal characteristic of letters. The former are apt, especially in non-Catholic countries, to assume various forms of " edification " and as one of these, following *The Confessions of St Augustine,* they first made their appearance in the book market. It is interesting to note, that the published journal came into fashion about the same time as the published letter, the *Journals* of Fox, Penn and Crisp all appearing in 1694 ; oddly enough in this connection we find here too some confusion between fact and fiction, as in the early history of all literary types. Fräulein Danielowski has, in a most interesting study, shown how the spiritual self-analyses of the early Quakers developed a regular literary form—and also how closely this literary form resembles the one Richardson chose for his *Pamela,* down even to the prefatory puffs and concluding summaries.

§ 5

The question, which has already been before us in a wider aspect, now presents itself again : how much did

Richardson know of and about the literature whose development and peculiarities have, very summarily, been sketched in the foregoing paragraphs ? Fräulein Danielowski declines to pronounce " for " any direct influence exerted by the Quaker autobiographers on the form of *Pamela.* Should the same caution condition the verdict on the more obvious novel-connection ? Richardson had heard of the *Arcadia* and, under the name of *Dorastus and Faunia,* of Greene's *Pandosto* : he makes several references to " Arcadian " things, besides probably deriving his first heroine's name from Sidney, and Mrs. Sinclair's cook was reading *Dorastus and Faunia* in bed on the night of the supposed fire at her house. *Grandison* contains a reference to the most successful English imitation of Mademoiselle de Scudéry's books, the *Parthenissa* of Roger Boyle, first Earl of Orrery. Mr. Brand in *Clarissa* makes mention of De Foe, whom he qualifies as " an ingenious man, though a *dissenter.*" Richardson evidently knew, too, what sort of thing a novel was, since Pamela naively, but justly exclaims : " Well, my story would surely furnish out a surprizing kind of novel, if it be well-told ; " and he very obviously adopted (and gave fresh life to) one general tradition associated with the romance and novel, that of using a complicated love-story for the staple—a tradition, however, he may equally well have derived from the plays he saw in his youth. But this is very nearly all that can be claimed for him as a student of fiction. If *Gulliver's Travels* be set on one side, there is no direct or indirect evidence in any of his books or letters that he had actually read any novel of older date than his own,—with one exception. That exception, however, is interesting and significant ; but no less interesting and significant is the obvious nature of

SAMUEL RICHARDSON

his reaction to that stimulus. Mrs. Shirley, a minor character in *Grandison*, repeats a bygone remonstrance of her friend Mrs. Eggleton :

"A Duke de Nemours : said she, taking up the *Princess of Cleves* that unluckily lay on my table—Ah, my Henrietta ! have I found you out ?—The princess, my dear, was a silly woman. Her story is written with dangerous elegance ; but the whole foundation of her distresses was an idle one. To fancy herself in love with a mere stranger, because he appeared agreeable at a ball, when she lived happily with a worthy husband, was mistaking mere *liking* for love, and combating all her life after the chimera of her own creating."

Clearly, for Mrs. Eggleton and, we may safely infer, for Richardson too *La Princesse de Clèves* had no aesthetic interest or interest of an exalted ethical character : it was merely an adulterous tale to be discountenanced ; and that disapproval was extended to all other productions of the kind. Virtuous Colonel Morden speaks indignantly of inflaming novels, and idle and improbable romances, that contribute to enervate and weaken women's minds. Richardson's own work was to have nothing in common with such. It is "a new species of writing, that might possibly turn young people into a course of reading different from the pomp and parade and romance-writing, and dismissing the improbable and marvellous with which novels generally abound, might tend to promote the cause of religion and virtue," as he said about *Pamela* ; and in the Postscript to *Clarissa* he equally rebukes those who consider that production " a mere *novel* or *romance*." In short, his new species, founded on Truth and Nature,

164

with hints for characters and situations occasionally derived from his own experience, was to owe nothing to a mischievous literary tradition, about which he knew but the vaguest generalities.[1]

Most literary historians would agree to the above. But a sub-variant of the general problem is often raised and presented in something like this form : " Granted that Richardson did not know his trashy predecessors at first hand, may he not have made mental reservations in favour of novels that were *not* inflaming or of romances that could not properly be summed up as idle and improbable, and, though he may not have read such, may he not have obtained some knowledge of them indirectly, through reading reviews and the like ? Is it not, for instance, likely that before he wrote of Pamela he had heard something about a similar young person, the heroine of Marivaux's *Marianne ?* " Fräulein Schroers, for one, insists on Richardson's friendship with literary men, on the curiosity with which, for instance, he questioned Mr. Lobb of Peterhouse : " Who now are your rising geniuses at Cambridge ?   What new works are in hand ? " and on the fact that other acquaintances, like Aaron Hill, had constant communication with the hives of literary gossip ; so that even if Richardson read very little of *belles-lettres*, he must have had a good superficial knowledge of what was going on in their realm.

It is impossible to prove a negative to all this and, more specifically, to disavow any and all connection with Marivaux.   Book-reviews, to be sure, cannot have helped our author to any extensive second-hand knowledge of

---

[1] Letters, however, interested him, and we find him commending those of Madame de Sévigné and Ninon de L'Enclos to Lady Bradshaigh.

fiction, since they were as bald as they were few and far between in the periodicals of his day. But the established fact that he knew no French is countered by the equally well-attested fact that a translation of *Marianne* began to appear in 1736 and that the work was popular enough in this country for three English versions to be called for within a decade. And, though Richardson's correspondence with literary men is rather barren of Grub Street gossip or aesthetic discussion, there is no knowing what may or may not have been said at the tea-tables of Salisbury Court and North End. Warburton may then have been justified in declaring in his preface to the first edition of *Clarissa* that the author of that work had deliberately proceeded on the " sensible Plan " in which some of the late writers of France had greatly excelled, when they substituted for the improbabilities of the older fiction " a faithful and chaste copy of real *Life and Manners*," and accordingly when Richardson expunged such direct allegations of his indebtedness from later editions of the book he was merely betraying a guilty conscience. It seems, however, more likely that the undoubted resemblances between Richardson's books and those of Marivaux and other contemporaries are due, not to deliberate borrowing, but the similar situations with which they deal and, in a greater degree, to the spirit and the general artistic temper of the age. Probably too the periodical essay which, we know, interested him and which Marivaux helped to popularize on the Continent may be accountable for certain particular features in the general resemblance. The situation is very similar to that of Richardson's relations to the development of the " epistolary technique." Richardson might possibly have got his hint from the *Lettres Portugaises* or Tom Brown's *Lindamira*, but it is equally

likely and better attested by the available evidence that
the technique of Pamela was suggested by his own work
on the *Familiar Letters*—the latter work in itself an
indication of the general interest taken in domestic writing,
which was satisfied on the one hand by Mrs. Manley
and her like and, on the other, by Steele and his successors
among the periodical essayists.

§ 6

Richardson's relations to his age, however, were not
without exception unconscious or semi-conscious like
those just considered. He may deliberately have averted
his gaze from contemporary literature, just hearing the
confused hum of commentary upon it, but on the morality
of the times he certainly kept it open and unswerving : in
fact, as we have seen, his neglect of letters was in part the
result of ethical predilection.

The state of popular morals in the first half of the
eighteenth century naturally shows the closest parallels
with the conditions obtaining in politics and literature.
Collier's attack on what we consider typical Restoration
drama, with its resounding echoes, implies one very close
connection. Steele, who had militantly endeavoured to
purify the stage, with equal resolution undertook to supply
a corrective to the loose social morality which contemporary comedy mirrored. And here, perhaps, he gained
the greater success : the compromise in matters of outlook
and behaviour which he advocated found more general
and lasting acceptance than the technique of *The Tender
Husband*. In the Preface to his *Christian Hero* (1710)
he pointed out that Men of Business carried less weight
in the commonwealth than they should, because they

lacked style and charm. But the body of this little work was addressed mainly to the other half of mankind, the Men of Wit, nurtured on classical ideals. By the example of celebrated heathens he showed that their philosophy, which derived its motives from " fame " or outward reputation, failed at supreme crises and that only a morality based on conscience could successfully pass the test in which Cato, Cæsar and Brutus had failed. " True greatness of mind," he concluded, " is to be maintain'd only on Christian principles ; " and these, as he goes on to expand, comprise, in addition to conscience, good-will, service and a humility that shall appear to spring rather from enlightened self-interest than ostentatious altruism.

Steele's dual programme, the Christianizing of the wits and the polishing of the puritans, was advocated also, though in blunter fashion, by De Foe and stated in a variety of forms both by Steele and Addison, in some of the most important papers of *The Tatler* and *The Spectator*. Lillo, characteristically enough, accepted a minimum of the compromise, confining himself to the advocacy of puritan virtues of the most obvious kind—honest dealing, plain speaking, industry and frugality, all strongly tinged with " class-consciousness "—and left the airs and graces, even those of the spirit, to look after themselves. At this point Richardson, generally found in agreement, parts company with him. The Good Man Sir Charles Grandison is in fact the embodiment in fiction of the new " gentleman," the Christian Hero begotten of Steele—though Trooper Dick would perhaps have been unregenerate enough to make a wry face at the antics and sentiments of his ghostly son. Sir Charles, as we have seen, only admitted the " monitor within " as a guide to his behaviour, his life was spent in promoting the interests of others and in perfecting himself in order to become more useful, and he always took great care to point out that what might look like arrant altruism was, in fact, dictated by entirely selfish considerations—not his fault, if no one would believe him ! In addition, he was a classical scholar, a patron and practitioner of the arts, an observer of men and their institutions who might well have made the Grand Tour with Addison himself.

Richardson indeed carried the ethical advance of Steele a couple of steps farther. First, he put forward as the criterion by which the true Christian gentleman might be tested his attitude towards women and his treatment of them, and it does not require any great ingenuity to find concrete exemplifications in all the three novels : Lovelace is put to the test and fails ; Mr. B—— redeems himself after a long period of trial ; Grandison always stands superior to the suggestion of any such test. Richardson advocated an abrogation of the old dual morality, with one code of sexual ethics for men and another, stricter one for women ; he demands that men should behave in their relations to persons of the other sex as they require women to do. The second part of his reforms concerned women more directly ; they were to be " levelled up " like the men, though elsewhere ; he virtually claimed that they should behave and be as they conventionally expected men to be : not silly, wanton, frivolous pets, with the vices of captivity, but self-reliant, useful members of a Christian community. We have seen that certain female emancipators of the time did not altogether approve of Richardson's pioneering, holding that he did not go far enough ; but perhaps they failed to realize that certain qualities, which he still advocated for women and which they considered to have been unduly impressed upon them in the past—self-effacement, domestic devotion and the like, were by him advocated for men also.

§ 7

These general manifestations of that even more general abstraction, the Spirit of the Age, are all correlated—by the various personal agents, for instance. They may also be systematized in diverse ways, one of which has been indicated. And, although it might be the effect of distortion to see them all merely as various phrases of that one ambiguous quality, it is undeniable that they are all, to a greater or less extent, permeated by sentimentalism.

If the term be used in its proper, neutral sense, it means a disposition to indulgence in the tenderer emotions and in the reflections which these emotions suggest or which conjure them up ; or it may mean that indulgence itself. Its principal *differentiæ* lie, first, in the intimate association between thought and feeling which it encourages, rumination and generalization upon the emotional data becoming as important as the experiences of them ; and, then, in the selection which it makes from the whole range of human emotions ; it rules out scorn, envy, malice and all uncharitableness, as well as all emotions, whether condemned by the moralist or not, when they occur in sufficient strength to warrant the use of the term passion. A person in whom sentimentalism is apparent, a sentimentalist, is one who more often than not indulges in *charity*, to use that term in its widest sense as comprising, in the definition of the *Concise Oxford Dictionary*, " Christian love of fellow men. . . ; kindness, natural affection . . . , candour, freedom from censoriousness, imputing of good motives when possible, leniency ; beneficence,

liberality to the poor, alms-giving. . . ." "Christian
love of fellow men" is essentially unselfish and inseparably
bound up with sympathy, the faculty of sharing emotions,
the most clearly defined variety of which is compassion
or pity. A sentimentalist, if he be sincere, will obviously
look upon the sentimental attitude of mind as the right
and good attitude, indeed the best, and accordingly exalt
sentiment above passion on the one hand and unemotional
thought on the other. Moreover, since his charity, as
we have read, commands him to impute good motives
when possible, he must hold that mankind in general is
actuated by the same excellent principles as himself and is
essentially charitable and altruistic, that is to say Good.
The last process in the development of this, as of all not
purely intellectual philosophies of life, is to look upon it
as Virtue *par excellence* and to inculcate its acceptance
and propagation as a *duty*.

A general theory such as this is often held and invariably
voiced by peoples and sections of society which aim at a
political independence or power which they do not as
yet enjoy. It guarantees the peaceableness and promises
the moral profit of a revolution in their favour. It is
that which prepares the way for the Robespierres and the
Lenins and is often preached by them. It was particularly appropriate that the English middle-class, the most
powerful of "oppressed peoples" in the seventeenth
century, should embrace it, since it so obviously accorded
with the Christian professions which were their chief
glory.

Now, during the times that we are considering, Christianity itself underwent everywhere in the West changes
which have the closest bearing on the development of
sentimentalism. After the settlement of the religious

balance of power with the peace of Westphalia, the frustration of Louis XIV's aggressive policy and the expulsion of the Stewarts, its militant phase was past. The Lord of Hosts might abdicate and the God of Love succeed. That such a thing did take place is evidenced by the growth of Pietism and Quakerism among the Protestants, and phenomena such as Madame Guyon's Quietism on the Roman side. The idea and conviction of Original Sin weakened together with the power of the jealous tyrant-god ; it ceased to be an axiom that " the heart of a man is deceitful above all things and desperately wicked ; " and those who rejected it (which they could soon do without moulting a feather of their orthodoxy) might safely concern themselves with the passions and emotions. Even Christian Puritanism could lose its rigour and produce *belles-lettres*. Nor did it need ever to move on the high altitudes of *The Pilgrim's Progress*. It could be softer and gentler without smelling of brimstone. The " feminine " period starts in religion and morals, and in literature which subserves them.

So it comes that sentimentalism becomes associated with the religious section *par excellence* of the population of the country, the puritan, trading, utilitarian middle-class. It seems doubtful whether the middle-classes, as such, are more prone to sentimentalism than any others ; indeed, their enemies have not been slow to cry out against an unholy paradox between their commercial activity (and the exploitation that often goes with it) and their emotionally tinged altruistic principles. The intimate alliance of middle-class supremacy in society and politics with sentimental art may be mainly a historical accident, though it must not be forgotten, on the other side of the argument, that Puritanism, of which commercial prosperity appears to be a function, has, in communities professing Christianity, obvious leanings towards sentimentalism.

Two historical circumstances tended to preserve and strengthen the sentimental view of life in this country, where those surrounding its origin had been so propitious. In the first place, after 1660 and 1688 the old order and the new continued to exist side by side—as they did not, for instance, in France after 1789 and in Russia after 1917—and the new, accordingly, neither had to fight very hard for bare life against the old nor attained complete mastery until mastery became a meaningless expression. It was on its best behaviour for so many generations that, to take the typical Cavalier view of the Roundhead, the wolf had kept on his sheep's clothing of sanctimonious canting until it had become part of his hide. In the second place, the sentimental view of life is one particularly suited to a society in the enjoyment of peace and a far-reaching prosperity ; in pioneers, warriors or beggars the tender emotions can only take a subordinate place. And perhaps the English people has never seen an age of better distributed, general affluence than that which attained its meridian in Walpole's ministry. The phenomenon of sentimentalism, as we shall see in the next chapter, was, with the word *sentimental*, transplanted from England to all countries of Europe. But it nowhere took firmer root than in its native soil ; in most lands, artificially fostered, it flourished but for a few seasons, and, where it has grown most luxuriantly and become a permanent feature in the moral landscape, as in Holland and Germany, it has constantly needed refreshing by grafts from the richly burgeoning old stock ;—for as such we may regard the successive waves of enthusiasm on the continent for the English Romanticists, for Dickens and for Mr. Galsworthy. Never was man farther out than John Wesley when, in his Journal for 11 February, 1772, he identified the new word " Sentimental " with " Continental."

§ 8

It is not the present purpose to isolate after painful analysis the elements which may be classed as sentimental in eighteenth century legislation, the growth of institutions, the new drama, the formless, goalless fiction of the reigns of Anne and George I, the gentlemanly ideal of Steele. Some of them should have become apparent in the short account of these topics just given. But it is necessary to dwell on some of the later developments of the sentimental principle in art and to study the relations subsisting between them and Richardson's work.

It may be observed how, to begin with, the sentimental spirit found a good deal in common with the classical spirit. The ideal of proportion and restraint, not unconnected with egalitarianism as well of the republican as of the Augustan kind, had in the course of the seventeenth century, with varying success in different countries, striven to oust the essentially aristocratic, hierarchic spirit of the preceding age. The sentimentalist, in the first, unspoiled period of sentimentalism, believed equally with the classic in " nothing too much : " for, in the thought-feeling complex that animates most of us most of the time, too much emotion means passion and too much thought may mean cynicism, or at least cold rationalism. Both the classic (the English-speaking classic in particular) and the sentimentalist laid also great store by the moral ingredient in art, the former because of his masters' precepts, the latter because of the ingrained utilitarianism of the class from which he sprang. Both disliked extravagance of all kinds. Both wanted art to deal with typical cases rather than idiosyncrasies, however interesting, partly from doctrinaire bias, since " rules " and not " exceptions " serve as the safer moral guides, and partly because both, for rather different reasons, wished the subject-matter of art to be comprehensible to the " average man " and amenable to the criticism of " Common Sense."

After a little while, however, sentimentalism and classicism begin to part company. A good deal of the responsibility for this split lies with the aristocrat, Lord Shaftesbury, the pupil of Locke. In his philosophy (promulgated 1711) the natural order constitutes a supreme harmony, which it is the privilege of man in his greatest moments of exaltation to perceive. Since the moral order is co-extensive with the natural, the harmony of the latter extends to the former as well. Those qualities, therefore, that in his moral nature man perceives to correspond with the harmonious Spirit of Nature are the more fundamental, and those that threaten this harmony are but perversions and distortions of his real, benevolent nature that craves for Virtue : as the universe contains no discordant, evil principle, so man's " sins " are merely failings or shortcomings, his vices a suspension or conflict (it may be) of his virtues. It is only necessary for mankind to give its real self free play in order to inaugurate the millennium of Harmony and Virtue. From such mystical optimism the classic must dissent, especially in the face of Shaftesbury's own declaration that, to an impartial view, the nature of human society would hardly seem to support his thesis of universal good. But the sentimentalist, not at all unfamiliar with mysticism and avid of reassurance, could more readily accept it : he welcomed his lordship for providing a philosophical foundation to his cardinal belief in the innate goodness of man. As a guarantee of man's altruism and an active, positive promoter of its exercise, he gratefully acknowledged the " moral or social sense " invented by Shaftesbury, although at first he was fain to pass over his counterbalancing repudiation of that negative principle of action, the Conscience, which had hitherto been deemed to hold sway in man's soul and which the Moral Sense was to replace. But that repudiation was bound eventually to become wide-spread in an age when all Authority was questioned and disparaged, when Newton and Locke had shaken the bases of thought as powerfully as Freud and Einstein have in our own. Ultimately, even so pliant an arbiter as the Moral Sense had to be discarded. " Je parviens à établir dans mon esprit comme des vérités primitives le néant de la vertu et la nécessité des passions," says a later novel-hero ; but he belongs to the last period of sentimentalism.

From Shaftesbury's time on, sentimentalism loses its philistine character and becomes more " enthusiastic," in the sense of the adjective then current, as is shown by three works published in 1746, Collins's *Ode on the Poetical Character*, Akenside's *Pleasures of the Imagination*, and Joseph Warton's *Enthusiast*. Concurrently, under the uncontrolled stimulus of the Moral Sense, the " sensibility " that had begun to accompany sentimentalism, becomes more extravagant. Sensibility, of course, at first meant nothing more than sensitiveness, though the term was usually restricted to mental feelings. Later it came to indicate an acute susceptibility to those emotions only which the sentimentalist exalted and, therefore, as commendable as acute. It might be carried to any lengths, with the result that you get your " sensible " person (who is also your " virtuous " person) reacting to the comparatively mild stimuli allowed by the sentimentalists to the full extent of his or her capacity : the love of brother and sister is expressed in terms not inappropriate to Antony and Cleopatra (hence, partly, the puzzling popularity of incest as a literary *motif* in the eighteenth century), the sight of an unknown dead donkey evokes tears that might grace a mother's bier, a village organist is described as if he were a Paganini, and the image of Golgotha has to do service for the most trivial inconvenience. The reaction, in a word, becomes all in all, the parade of it a guarantee of its actuality, and the " value" of the stimulus, together with all other " values ", sinks into unimportance.

In the course of time a sentimental code also comes into being, which still further detracts from the estimableness of the outpourings. Certain stimuli, it is postulated, should in every truly sensible person evoke certain reactions, and these accordingly are simulated or represented as occurring, even when they do not or cannot exist. To take but a few obvious examples : according to the provisions of the code, the meeting of blood-relations engenders joys and the paramount residuum after this joy has spent itself is the emotion of love ; old age demands (and therefore receives) reverence, misfortune, pity ; the sight of death is afflicting and the news of it only a degree less so ; the idea of divine worship calls forth awe ; and so on. It does not matter whether the blood-relationship be unknown to the parties chiefly concerned or be shown, on rational reflection, to entail highly vexatious conse-

quences, whether old age have nothing extrinsic deserving
of veneration, whether failure be well deserved, whether
death have been inflicted by the witness of it in the heat
of anger or combat, whether the news of it comes to the
hearing of complete strangers or of persons whose interests
are favourably affected by it, whether the chapel be but
an "elegant apartment" set aside for "prayers;"—
the code itself decrees that nothing shall impede the
reactions which it prescribes. Again it is the reaction,
that is to say the emotional indulgence and parade, irrespective of all circumstances and ulterior causes, which
possesses the paramount importance. Another provision of sentimentalism deals with Delicacy. If a man's
feelings be regarded as sacred, they must be approached
with the reverent awe befitting a sanctuary : hence those
endless *ménagements* and misunderstandings, due to the
wish to avoid hurting or exciting the feelings with which
sentimental literature, in France especially, abounds.
Of course the development and progressive insincerity of
this sentimental code received a great impetus from
Shaftesbury's *Characteristics*, since exaltation was there
celebrated as the highest mental state ; but the mixture
of duty with emotion, which is found of the essence of
sentimentalism from its first beginnings, ensured its
emergence at an earlier date.

In connection with the parade of sensibility it may
perhaps come most appropriately to mention the physiological phenomenon most generally associated with sentimentality, that of weeping. Tears, indeed, are not only
natural, but also invaluable to the sentimentalist : on the
one hand, they are only a degree less easy to call up than
to "conceal;" on the other, they are, by common consent, the appropriate physiological reaction to many of

precisely those gentle feelings to which he should show himself a prey : the unadulterated passions rarely call them forth, still less frequently unemotional thoughts. To shed them, therefore, can give rise to no unworthy suspicion ; they are, indeed, a badge of virtue, like indulgence, nay, wallowing in sentimental emotion of any kind.

The popularity of tears in a sentimental society and in sentimental art accounts, perhaps, for the comparative popularity of death. Death, mourning and weeping form so unexceptionable a causal chain, that even an undesirable visitor like the King of Terrors may be welcomed for the irrefutable proofs of inherent virtue which his presence calls forth among his hosts. But anyhow death is an obvious sentimental theme, on account of the emotion it naturally evokes in everybody and of the various moralizing reflections which it equally naturally suggests in all who feel the experience not too poignantly. The same may be said of decay in general, of which death is but one aspect ; and on this Mr. Michael Sadleir, speaking of the latter eighteenth century, has a valuable observation : " To the Gothistic age, however, a ruin was itself a thing of loveliness—and for interesting reasons. A mouldering building is a parable of the victory of nature over man's handiwork."

§ 9

Richardson is a sentimentalist of the older school. His books reveal no direct trace of Shaftesbury's doctrines ; and on the one occasion on which that nobleman is mentioned, execration is his part. Grandison, to take an illustration of cardinal significance, called his guiding principle a " monitor : " it is the repressive agent, Con-

science ; and this Christian, Protestant principle of
Conscience forms the moral core of Clarissa and Pamela,
and of the Papist Clementina too. Hand in hand with
his championship of Conscience goes Richardson's distrust of impulse (remember what happened to Clary
Harlowe !) and of " enthusiasm," at any rate where it is
called by that name. Says Grandison, the author's
mouthpiece, to Dr. Bartlett : " Religion and love, Dr.
Bartlett, which heighten our relish for the things of both
worlds, what pity is it that they should ever run the human
heart into enthusiasm or superstition ; and thereby debase
the minds they are both so well fitted to exalt." (Against
this it may be observed that Methodism, the " enthusiastic"
doctrine *par excellence* during the seventeen-forties and
'fifties, receives gentler handling from Richardson than
from most other men of letters at the time. No doubt
he rightly valued it more by its reiteration of sternly
puritanical doctrines, the insistence on damnation for
instance, than by the excesses of some of its more negligible devotees.) Certainly neither he nor any of his
creatures can attain to ecstasies, let alone to that state of
exaltation in which Shaftesbury bids man adore the
universal harmony : indeed they would have thought it
indecorous to attempt such a thing and indecent to wish
for it. Though there may be some rhetoric, we search
in vain through Richardson's pages for any truly lyrical
effusion : even when unfettered by prosodical laws, he
hardly advanced into this realm beyond the halting stutter
of Pamela's artless verses. Horses are not to be docked,
nor flowers plucked ; but there are no celebrations of the
majesty or mysteriousness of nature, man's mystic union
with her, or of the strange, intoxicating and negligible
microcosm which he carries within his own breast.

Yet to the emancipatory effect which Shaftesbury's teaching, beginning with James Thomson, had on poets and lovers of literature his work bears some slight witness. We have noted that he reprobated Pope's and Swift's cynicism and lamented that talents which might have redounded to the glory of humanity were employed to baser uses ; how, as an off-set, the more emotional poets, some of them languishing in unfashionable neglect, received commendation, though he still inclined to rank Addison above Shakespeare.

At the same time, as his upbringing would lead one to expect, his attitude towards classicism in its official guise is hostile. References to and quotations from the Moderns greatly preponderate over those taken from the Ancients. The only fairly important character in his books who can be identified absolutely with the older education and learning, Mr. Elias Brand of *Clarissa*, is deliberately rendered unamiable and ridiculous, while Harriet Byron confounds a champion of the classics by citing first Milton and then Addison. And it seems to be Lillo whom Pamela, ingeniously wise before the foregone conclusion, has in mind when she pronounces on theatrical reform :

" I think the stage, by proper regulations, might be made a profitable amusement. . . . The terror and compunction for evil deeds, the compassion for a just distress, and the general beneficence which those lively exhibitions are so capable of raising in the human mind, might be of great service, when directed to right ends, and induced by proper motives : Particularly where the actions which the catastrophe is designed to punish are not set in such advantageous lights as shall destroy the end of the moral, and make the vice that ought to be censured, imitable ; where instruction is kept in view all the way ; and where vice is punished, and virtue rewarded."

In these small particulars Richardson inclined to the programme of the more radical among the sentimental revolutionaries. For the rest, however, he is as perfect a representative as could be wished of the older, sober-sided stalwarts. He has no doubt that he and his kind make up the salt of the earth and lets his aristocratically-connected and aristocratically-minded Lovelace exclaim : " were it not for the *poor* and the *middling*, the world would, probably, long ago, have been destroyed by fire from Heaven." Harriet Byron objects to her sister-in-law's using the word *cit*, with its customary associations, " in a trading kingdom," and Sir Charles Grandison, though by no means one of them, declares that the " merchants of Great Britain are the most useful members of that community." His lady cries out contemptuously against Honour, the " noble " counterpart to Conscience and the Moral Sense : " Murderous, vile word *honour !* What . . . is honour ? The very opposite to duty, goodness, piety and religion, and to everything that is or ought to be sacred among men." The whole of *Clarissa* may, indeed, be regarded as a lengthy parable on the antithesis of the aristocratic and familiar codes, to demonstrate the superiority of the latter. In his detestation of what are called the heroic virtues, to which honour is so nearly associated, Richardson actually copies the language and illustrations of his abhorred rival, the author of *Jonathan Wild the Great.* Lovelace writes to Belford of Julius Cæsar—for whom Richardson elsewhere professed comparatively fair respect :

" Cæsar, we are told, had won, at the age of fifty-six,

when he was assassinated, fifty pitched battles, had taken
by assault above a thousand towns, and slain near 1,200,000
men ; I suppose exclusive of those who fell on his own
side in slaying them.   Are not you and I, Jack, innocent
men, and babes in swaddling-clothes, compared to Cæsar,
and to his predecessor in heroism, Alexander, dubbed, for
murders and depredation, *Magnus ?* "

And Harriet Byron calls out : " What is the boasted
character of most of those who are called HEROES, to
the unostentatious merit of a TRULY GOOD MAN ! "
    Harriet Byron ejaculates further : " But what an
absurdity is this passion called love ?   Or rather, of what
absurd things does it make its votaries guilty ?   Let mine
be evermore circumscribed by the laws of reason, of
duty ; " and Sir Charles puts the wider rhetorical question : " To what purpose live we, if not to grow wiser,
and to subdue our passions ? "
    Richardson extends his animosity against passion,
against heroism, against honour, against the aristocracy
and classical learning even to beauty itself.   In a revolting
passage of a letter to Miss Wescomb he wishes—" in
charity " too—that the two meteoric beauties of the day,
the Misses Gunning, might get their faces seamed with
the small-pox and so realize the nothingness of their
natural endowments.   And his fundamental puritanism
is further shown in the causes he alleges for the fall of
Polly Horton, the prostitute : music, songs, romances,
novels and plays.
    But everything that has been said about Richardson so
far should have shown him as profuse in the advocacy and
illustration of the principles that met with his approval as
in his condemnation of those he deemed pernicious ; and

so we shall find him here. Conduct was his prime concern, and no conduct in his opinion could be right if it were not based on feeling. " The Goodness of the Heart, so much preferable to the Head alone," he exclaims in a letter to Aaron Hill. And Clarissa, here unmistakably speaking for the author too, says : " I would reject the man with contempt, who sought to suppress, or offered to deny, the power of being visibly affected upon *proper* occasions, as either a savage-hearted creature, or as one who was ignorant of the principal glory of the human nature, as to place his pride in a barbarous insensibility." Once more Cato stands condemned, and it is to Christian doctrine that Richardson, like Steele, turns for his principles of action.

The milder and most specifically Christian virtues of Pity, Charity and Humility, with a Duty so closely allied to Inclination as to have lost almost all its sternness, are indeed inculcated in almost every letter that he wrote. The definition of Charity quoted from the *Concise Oxford Dictionary* might have been framed after no more than an analysis of the single character of Sir Charles Grandison, the servant of the inner monitor. To have pointed to Pamela Andrews in her round-eared cap and to have said in so many words : " Behold the Handmaiden of God," Richardson would doubtlessly and rightly have considered the height of indecorum ; but the veneration which he accorded her and endeavoured (with much success) to raise in others on her behalf indicates an inner conviction from which such an exclamation would hardly have seemed to come as an inappropriate salutation. Clarissa too, a maid and not a maid, outcast and humilated, refrains from all outcry, from all but the gentlest, indirect self-exculpation and from the prosecution of all revenge, to die resigned in the quiet faith that had sustained her. She is, as the author claimed, "a truly *Christian heroine,*" the deliberately constructed counterpart of Steele's Christian Hero.

Sensibility, however, though never attaining to " enthusiasm " is pretty well developed. With it Richardson endowed all (or almost all) his characters, he confidently expected it in his public (nor was he disappointed) and he himself possessed it : at giving away another man's daughter in marriage at St. George's, Hanover Square, he was so excited that he could not hold a pen for days together. The very tenor of his books, written in the belief that the petty happenings retailed in them would engage the attention at least as closely as an account of the vastest exploits, whether real or imagined, together with his direct appeal to the emotions, really furnishes sufficient proof ; and it should be clinched by his dictum : " Sensibility is the principal glory of the human nature." But a word may still be said in illustration of the excessive tearfulness of his characters and of the excessive fondness (as it appears to us) with which they dwell on death. Tears are the tokens by which they may arrogate unto themselves superiority over the brute creation : when the excellent and gallant Colonel Morden gives way to them he paraphrases them as "a repeated fit of humanity." Lovelace is the only character of any importance drawn by Richardson who has them not always at command (a proof in itself, if any further were needed, of his moral perversity), and yet even he, when he deliberately *invents* and retails a cock-and-bull story of a pending reconciliation between Clarissa and her family and witnesses her joy, confesses that he " *audibly* sobbed "—which however, stirred him no further to humanity, since he kept up the cruel imposture. In *Grandison* the general humidity, a sign of the advancing times maybe, seems greater than in the tragedy of *Clarissa*, and the greatest precipitation is attained, naturally enough from sentimental considerations, in the long-protracted report of the dissolution of Sir Charles's mother, who exclaims with macabre satisfaction : " You embalm, my son, with your tears—Oh how precious the balm." A parallel to this is to be read in the observation of Clarissa's elderly friend, Mrs. Judith Norton, to the effect that having her eyes closed in death by Clarissa was a " pleasure " she had so often " promised" to herself.

§ 10

Here perhaps, in the opinion of some, we may discern already the operation of what has been called " the Sentimental Code," with the inevitable insincerity that flows from it. " What," such censors ask, " is Lady Grandison the elder to us, or even to Harriet Byron (who never knew her), that Richardson should make her and us snivel over the second-hand account of her death-bed ? And should not Mrs. Norton receive rather the contempt reserved for all dotards than tearful applause for her resigned and Christian fortitude ? " It may be that such cavilling proceeds from a healthier attitude of mind than that on which Richardson had relied. But in fairness to him, it may be said that he rarely lays himself open to criticisms of this kind. That well-developed realism of his saved him from many pitfalls into which many of his successors, with a looser grasp on actuality, too often lapsed. Common-sense, unless it disapproves of the pathetic and tragic in themselves, is not often outraged or credulity strained, as it may be by the instance just given or by the spectacle of contrite Harlowes to the end of their days using the back-stairs so as to avoid passing their martyr'd kinswoman's room. And, again, though Richardson may have rendered his characters unduly sensitive to sentimental stimuli, unduly prone to administer them to themselves and preternaturally careful of the feelings of others, and though he may have considered their hypertrophied sensibility desirable for mankind at large, he rarely made himself guilty of trying to make others sensitive to *unworthy* stimuli, or a prey to the softer emotions and to false delicacy where robuster feelings and actions would seem more suitable. Perhaps Fielding was right when he insinuated that chastity like Pamela's and repentance like Mr. B——'s were not worth making such a song about ; perhaps some of the worthier members of the community would feel warmer emotions for Clarissa if she had boldly laid information against Mr. Lovelace ; we are certainly not impressed by the tragic emotions alleged to labour in the latter's bosom on hearing that he proposes to wear out his days in the company of a golden casket, containing Clarissa's pickled heart ; but the emotions and principles underlying the actions and states criticized are respectable, the occasions by no means trumpery. In general, when we are bidden to weep, it is for the death or discomfiture of the worthy, when we are bidden to stand amazed, it is at beholding their fortitude in real affliction, when we are bidden to rejoice, it is in the triumph of their perseverance. Richardson does not ask us to lament the death of Eugene Aram, as Lytton does, or hold that gambling to excess is pardonable if allied to warmth of heart, like Edward Moore, or applaud a miscarriage of justice which favours two arrant scoundrels who happen to be in love with one another, as in Aphra Behn's *Fair Jilt*.

No, Richardson's sentimentalism cannot fairly be condemned on such grounds.   What is much more exceptionable than the violence of the emotions portrayed or the value of the occasions which call them forth, is that *parade* of feeling and of the virtue with which it is identified, the inculcation of emotional effusiveness as a duty and its deliberate application to practical ends (here of a moral nature), which this generation, nurtured by propaganda, has come to look upon as the greatest of evils. There is a frigidity and a self-righteousness about it which combine to raise grave doubts about the sincerity and essentially unselfish nature of the sentimentalists' cardinal principle.   When old Andrews in his grief at the supposed ruin of his daughter comes humbly for news to the Lincolnshire mansion, Mr. B—— and the neighbouring gentry think it most proper that the affecting meeting between father and daughter should, for purposes of edification, take place publicly—as it accordingly does. But even that is less nauseating, since the scene is not set by the principal actors in it, than Harriet Byron's confession to a friend that in all her conduct she is governed by her aim at giving a tacit example to Emily Jervois— surely, Sir Charles's fear of Dr. Bartlett is a more respectable motive for virtuous behaviour than that !

This strange kind of theatrical ostentation which was thought to increase the estimability of the emotion and of the soul laid bare, as well as to add to the impressiveness of the display, is best illustrated by that marvellous letter of congratulation in the " lapidary style " which Clementina della Porretta sent to the Grandisons at their marriage and which later, no doubt, was suitably engraved on marble in the Temple of Friendship set up in their grounds :

Best of men ! ⎫
Best of women !⎰ Be ye *one*.
CLEMENTINA wishes it !
GRANDISON, lady, will make you happy.
Be it *your* study to make *him* so !—
Happy, as CLEMENTINA would have made him,
Had not obstacles invincible intervened.
This will lessen her regrets :
For,
His felicity, temporal and eternal,
Was ever the wish next her heart.
GOD be merciful to you both,
And lead you into His paths :
Then will everlasting happiness be your portion.
Be it the portion of CLEMENTINA—
Pray for her !—
That after this transitory life is over,
She may partake of heavenly bliss :
And
(Not a stranger to you, lady, HERE)
Rejoice with you both HEREAFTER,

CLEMENTINA DELLA PORRETTA.

§ 11

There is nothing very new or extreme in Richardson's sentimentalism itself. Much the same quality had already been introduced into literature by Steele, Lillo

189

and others, and it was to be carried to much more remarkable lengths by various authors considered in the next chapter. What stands out on retrospect more than its novelty and exuberance is the successful manner in which the author amalgamated it with other qualities and the skill with which he developed it to the furthest point compatible with these other qualities. There was one particular sphere where he realized that the combination of qualities at his command—his pathos, his psychological insight and his realism in conjunction with his sentimentalism—could enjoy the fullest scope : and that was the domestic. With his friend Aaron Hill he held :

> " Empires o'erturned, and heroes held in chains,
> Alarm the mind, but give the heart no pains.
> To ills remote from our domestic fears,
> We lend our wonder, but withhold our tears."

Accordingly Richardson made himself the laureate of the Christian family. On the sentimental basis, which the Behns and Barkers had used for frivolous or sensational or purely homiletic purposes, he erected, almost unaided, the domestic novel.

In the Christian family Richardson saw a microcosm of Christian society. " Does He not," asks Sir Charles Grandison during one of his speculations upon the deity, " interest Himself, if I may so express myself, in the performance of the filial duty ? May it not be justly said, that to obey your parents is to serve God ? " To prevent the most blatant kind of disruption of the hallowed circle Richardson even pretends a form of taboo : Belford writes to his boon companion, Lovelace : " Adultery is so capital a guilt, that even rakes and libertines disavow and condemn it,"—a palpably insincere piece of rhetoric for the benefit of the general public, since Lovelace, on his own showing, by no means " disavowed " the practice. The confusion of values accompanying sentimentalism enabled Richardson often to give a domestic tinge to what lay outside the domestic sphere—his ultimate wish no doubt being to include all the reformed world in one large and rather stuffy family circle. Honorary blood-relationships, with emotional reactions implied as a matter of course just as much as privileges are, abound to an almost startling extent in his writings. In *Grandison* alone we find Harriet entering into such relations with Sir Roland Meredith and his nephew, with Sir Charles (in the first part of the book) and his sisters, with Lady D—— (who wishes her to marry her son) and with a Mr. Orme, while Sir Charles does so with Mr. Orme too, with all the Porrettas and with his future wife.

To the peculiar appeal at which Richardson aimed the domestic note added the last persuasiveness. The new middle-class public, he had declared in effect, must have a new literature worthy of them, which should embody and advocate new standards of behaviour and art, to supplant the old, effete standards, just as the new social order was ousting the old. When the new doctrine was examined, the public, already flattered by the author's implied proposal to share his apostleship with them, was still more exquisitely flattered to find that it was nothing unheard-of or subversive in Lord Shaftesbury's style, but, for the most part, what had been handed down to them from pious forebears as their most valuable and distinctive heritage ; and, greatest flattery of all, the precious treasure was shown as requiring no more effective setting than the background of the daily life which they led or, without presumption, might all hope some day to lead. In revealing to them Virtue, he revealed *their* Virtue. So, at any rate, with a pardonable blindness to their own faults, they could readily believe. Such a nicely adjusted compromise between the strange and the familiar, between conservatism and radicalism, when made by a great artist could not but produce highly interesting effects.

Chapter Six

THE CONSEQUENCES OF RICHARDSON

§ 1

With his poor opinion of the age, Richardson was by no means confident that he had hit its taste with his domestic and romantic, sentimental, realistic and moralizing work. Accordingly, he valued the copyright of *Pamela* at no more than thirty guineas and disposed of two-thirds thereof *pro rata* to Osborn and Rivington. But its success was instantaneous and, for the time, remarkable. Five editions of the first two volumes appeared within a twelvemonth ; then came two editions of *Pamela in her Exalted Condition*, the third of which is described as the sixth for Volumes I and II. A gentleman at Oxford writes even of the less worthy concluding volumes : " all the Senior and more intelligent Part of the University highly value and esteem them. Two or three Fellows of Colleges my Acquaintance, Men eminent for their Learning and Good Sense, are full of their Praises every time I see them." From a dissentient remark of Hurd's we may indeed infer that Part II of *Pamela* was, with all its imbecilities, actually preferred to Part I. The author of the *Lettre sur Pamela* says that that work was a necessary piece of furniture in every genteel drawing-room.

SAMUEL RICHARDSON

The students of literature appreciated its significance at once, one of them writing to the author before the publication of the second edition that "This little Book will infallibly be looked upon as the hitherto much-wanted Standard and Pattern for this kind of Writing." The bibliophiles, however, seem to have furnished an exception to the universal enthusiasm : the sixth edition (January 1742) was something in the nature of an *édition de luxe*, octavo instead of duodecimo, with some slight alterations in the text and a series of copper-plates by Gravelot and Hayman ; but enough of the sheets for this remained in hand for a re-issue, still called the "sixth edition, corrected" and containing all the original advertisements, as late as 1772 ! By this time, the tenth edition had (1771) already appeared—not counting Irish editions and the like.

Clarissa and *Grandison* cost about double what had been asked (twelve shillings) for the completed *Pamela*. It is not surprising, therefore, to discover that they went off the booksellers' hands more slowly. But still sales and reception were extraordinary : Young could tell his friend, " I have read Clarissa thrice, and the last kiss was the sweetest ; " and by June 1751, two-and-a-half years after completion of the first edition, Richardson reported to a friend that he had disposed of nearly three thousand sets, the average price of which must have been over a guinea. In that year the third (duodecimo) and fourth (octavo) editions, containing fresh matter equivalent to a volume in bulk and embodying the definitive text, were issued. The sixth edition appeared in 1768, two years before the sixth edition of *Grandison*, which, it will be remembered, had started with a time-handicap of six years—which suggests that in its day and in

England *Clarissa* proved the least popular of the three books.[1]

Literary adaptations and imitations were as natural consequences of such popularity as the burlesques of which some mention has been made. Richardson counted sixteen " Remarks, Imitations, Retailings, Pyracies &c." called forth by *Pamela* alone. Some, like *Shamela* and *Joseph Andrews*, have already received notice. Among the rest no less than three " Anti-Pamelas ", which it is easy to confuse : namely, *The True Anti-Pamela : or Memoirs of Mr. James Parry* (a genuine autobiography, it seems, which ran through at least three editions and first appeared in 1741 or 1742) ; *Anti-Pamela : or Feign'd Innocence detected : In a Series of Syrena's Adventures* (1741, an originally English work, possibly written by Mrs. Haywood and translated into French in 1743) ; and *Antipamela ou Memoires de M. D——* (1742, which, though published in London, does not seem to be a translation and is certainly quite distinct from the other two books). All these books deal with heroines in whom chastity is by no means the ruling passion, insinuating at the same time that they are much more typical of womankind than Miss Andrews.

Equally obnoxious to the moralist must have been the knowledge that his Pamela had made her appearance upon the stage. In 1742, according to the *Biographia Dramatica*, two theatrical versions of her story appeared in print ; one, anonymous, was never acted ; the other by James Dance had been presented at the theatre in

[1] One may note for comparison : *Joseph Andrews*, first published in December 1741, reached its 9th edition in 1769 ; *Tom Jones* (April 1749), 7th edition 1768 ; *Amelia* (edition of 8,000 copies in 1751) had no further English edition before 1775, except in complete issues of Fielding's Works.

Goodman's Fields, London, on 9 November of the previous year. It is a fairly faithful, if crude dramatization of the First Part of the novel. A male pendant to the ill-bred fine lady, Lady Davers, was introduced in Jack Smatter, taken by an anonymous gentleman who is said to have written the part as well as the prologue to the play. This was none other than David Garrick, appearing again within three weeks of his remarkable *début* as Richard III at the same house.

The reception with which *Pamela's* successors met was free of such grossly discordant elements. A burlesque of *Clarissa* must needs have taken the form of cynical pornography, and it is as fanciful to look upon the celebrated *Fanny Hill*, published in 1749, as an "Anti-Clarissa," as to suppose with M. Digeon that Fielding fashioned his incontinent, but healthy and amiable hero in *Tom Jones* as a corrective to the morbid satanism, the sentimental remorse and the complete caddishness of Lovelace. To satirize *Grandison* would have required the genius of a Cervantes, a stature to which Smollett, the greatest novelist alive at the time of its completion, hardly attained ; moreover, the tide of popular taste was now running so strongly on the flood of sentimentality that even a Cervantes might have renounced any scheme of parody as predestined to failure. Grandison, it would appear, never made his way on to the boards of his native land either, and it was 1788 before a dramatization of *Clarissa* appeared.

§ 2

It is patent that an author who enjoyed success like Richardson's must have inspired many to follow him and,

with these followers, have left an impress upon the literature and thought of his country. Even after making all
allowance for the anonymous actions of the *Zeitgeist,*
great influence must still be attributed to him personally.
For one thing, he lent the prestige of his own aims and
accomplishment to the literary form which he had adopted.
In and after his time the novel takes rank among the
greater literary genera, as it had never and nowhere done
before. This, indeed, is part of a vaster achievement :
Richardson made the imagination and works of the
imagination respectable and, by so doing, brought them
into the ken of a large new public, as well as into the
conversation of others who had previously kept their
indulgence a secret. Adam Smith would no longer be
thought a crank when he affirmed that the " poets and
romance writers, who best paint the refinements and
delicacies of love and friendship, and of all other private
and domestic affections, Racine and Voltaire, Richardson,
Maurivaux, and [Mme. de] Riccoboni, are, in such cases,
much better instructors than Zeno, Chrysippus, and
Epictetus."

There is, again, a danger of claiming too much for any
one man, but it appears equally plainly that Richardson
had an active part in that great expansion of the book-
market during his lifetime, which allowed for great
co-operative undertakings like Smollett's *Histories* and
the encyclopædias and which made men of letters self-
supporting : it was his friend Johnson, it will be remembered, who broke with the patron in this country, just as
his contemporary and fellow-novelist, Marivaux, did in
France. The writers of the Napoleonic and Victorian
Ages—the Macaulays and Huxleys, no less than the
Scotts and Dickenses—consequently could appeal to

thousands where Johnson, Milton and Dryden, while they lived, could only appeal to scores ; the man of letters really could become Carlylean prophet and tribune of the people.

At the same time as he made Imagination free of a steadily growing number of counting-houses and the drawing-rooms above them, Richardson saw to it that she came a sober-suited matron pretending some other errand than that of merely giving pleasure. He counselled her to keep her wits about her and refrain from eye-rolling frenzies, to know all about the details of everyday life and to delight in dwelling on the little tricks of behaviour that most of her new acquaintances had in common ; he urged her, as much as possible, to look on the world through their windows or, at any rate, to describe it in terms familiar to those who had enjoyed no other outlook. In other words, he laid the foundations, more solidly than Steele or De Foe or Lillo had done, of realistic middle-class literature.

Equally naturally and firmly he established the not unnatural alliance of domesticity and sentimentalism, for the dissolution of which after the progress of four generations Ibsen toiled, but which not even Mr. Shaw has finally accomplished, and his practice countenanced that more strained connection of domesticity with romanticism or sensationalism, the fruits of which were first exploited by Mrs. Radcliffe and some of her companion Novelists of Terror—later by Dickens and all his tribe. He perfected the convention of a love-story as the staple of most imaginative works and gave a new importance to the heroine of it. He confirmed too the didactic and moralizing bent which classicism had imposed on literature, though to be sure, he gave it a new direction. It is clear, for instance, that Crabbe is a didactic poet just as much as Pope is, but one of the main differences between the quality of the two didacticisms lies in that pawkily sentimental element with which Richardson most heavily impregnated the body of literature.

It is the purpose of the rest of this study to describe certain aspects of these complicated processes.

§ 3

In poetry, naturally enough, Richardson's influence is furthest to seek : the seeds for the new harvest which the bloody years of the Revolution and the Napoleonic wars were to ripen were not sown by him, even though they might be by men between whom and him a reciprocal feeling of kinship existed—Thomson, Young and Gray, for instance. It is in the drama and, of course, in prose fiction that we must look for the most obvious and indisputable traces of his example and precept.

In the drama, single or associated elements popularized by Richardson constantly appear, both where we might expect them and where we would not. As an example of the latter, *Biographia Dramatica* describes, of all things, a burlesque for puppets written by Samuel Foote and presented by him at the Haymarket on 15 February, 1773, but never (it would seem) printed. The kinship to *Pamela* of *The Handsome Housemaid ; or, Piety in Pattens* will not need demonstration after the following account :

" The piece was of two acts ; the story of a servant-girl whose master had fallen in love with her ; and being offered a settlement by him, is warned by Thomas the

SAMUEL RICHARDSON

Butler, who loves her, and tells her to beware of her
master ; for if she once loses her virtue, she will have no
pretensions to chastity. She takes his advice, and slights
her master, who, overcome by her honest principles, and
the strength of his passion, offers to marry her : she begs
Thomas may be by, to hear the reply she gives to such a
noble offer ; when she immediately bestows her hand on
the Butler for counselling her so well. The Squire,
vanquished by such goodness, gives his consent to their
junction ; when the heroine, out of gratitude for his
great condescension, resolves to marry neither, and to
live single, although she loves them both."

Another free version of the same story is found in
Isaac Bickerstaff's *Maid of the Mill* (1765), which enjoyed a vogue sufficient to warrant six printed editions.
The author very freely acknowledged his indebtedness to
Pamela, not only for the subject in general, but also for
" almost every circumstance in it." In this he did himself less than justice, since the cardinal situation is radically
altered by substituting Lord Aimworth, a man of honour
imbued with recollections of *Arcadia* and Rousseau's
ideals, for the mixture of folly, caddishness and sensuality
known as Mr. B——— : the heroine, Patty, consequently
has to put up no defence of her honour, which Lord
Aimworth never jeopardises. Bickerstaff's piece was
a ballad opera or musical comedy of the kind which *The
Beggar's Opera* (1728) had made popular. From this
time forward Misalliance between a girl of lowly origin
and a fine gentleman (with and without the insinuation
that there may be, or nearly was, " an easier way ")
becomes pre-eminently *the* theme for musical comedy,
as the repertoire of the New Gaiety Theatre in its heyday,

200

with its *Shop Girl* and *Our Miss Gibbs*, testifies. Some of this, credit or debit as you choose, must be booked to Samuel Richardson.

On sentimental comedy in which music played no part, or a quite subordinate one, the influence of Richardson's art was more direct and obvious. Edward Moore, a friend of his (for all his shockingly outspoken remarks on *Clarissa*), had meditated dramatizing that story and, in his *Foundling* (1748), developed after his own fashion one of its cardinal situations. In it, the rake Belmont loves the friendless Fidelia and she him, but he suffers from the same moral itch as Lovelace in his determination to stick at no baseness in isolating her from her friends and then outraging her. He is foiled, contritely offers marriage, and is properly rejected. Then, however, the elders take a hand in the game and make it end with the customary pairing of the protagonists. There are two direct references to *Pamela* in *The Foundling*, and Fidelia's early mischances with one Villiard are reminiscent of Mr. B——'s thwarted assaults. In this play, too, we find the juxtaposition of airy and serious heroine, which perhaps goes back to *Much Ado About Nothing* and which Steele certainly provided with Lucinda and Indiana of *The Conscious Lovers*, but which received much encouragement from Miss Howe and Clarissa Harlowe and thereafter became a stock feature in drama. *The Foundling* appeared at the end of a period of about fifteen years singularly barren of good plays. It heralded a new florescence of sentimental comedy, which, constantly stimulated by sentimental fiction, becomes from the 1760's onwards a recognized literary form, with a continuous development, instead of the series of sporadic experiments that it had been during the previous two generations. After the protest of Sheridan's three great plays (1775-9), it held the field of comedy without a competitor for upwards of a hundred years.

§ 4

We proceed now to Richardson's own domain, the novel. Here the force of his example and purpose is of incalculably great strength. It is hardly an exaggeration to declare that no novel written after the appearance of *Pamela* was not in some way, either of imitation or repulsion, directly or indirectly affected by it and its successors from the same hand. Not even Fielding could avoid being sucked into Richardson's wake : who will deny that *Amelia* would have been a very different book, indeed might never have been written, but for *Pamela* and Richardson's pioneer-work in domestic literature ? Nor did the popular writers, whom many years' service prior to 1740 had confirmed in outlook, technique and favour, pursue the tenor of their old ways. Indeed the change in their work is the most eloquent testimony available to the new standard which Richardson had set in fiction.

Mrs. Davys, who described herself as " in years " in 1725, put forth as late as 1756 a novel entitled *The Accomplish'd Rake*. This, to be sure, greatly resembles her earlier books, but also seems to owe something to Smollett—and he was inspired by the example of Fielding, whose faculties as a novelist were sharpened by temperamental opposition to Richardson's morality. Moreover, *The Accomplish'd Rake* has a feature destined to enjoy great popularity for some decades—the undoing of the virtuous heroine with the help of an opiate : and this *motif* (as the Germans call such things) comes direct from Richardson and his *Clarissa*.

A better example of the changes wrought by Richardson's works in old stagers is afforded by the writings of Mrs. Eliza Haywood. This lady had begun her immensely prolific career in 1719, the year of *Robinson Crusoe*, and had, it is interesting to note, experimented with epistolary technique in *Love-Letters on All Occasions lately passed between Persons of Distinction* (1730). After *Pamela* and *The Familiar Letters* a definitely didactic element becomes apparent in her work, as in *Epistles for the Ladies* (1749) on the one hand and, on the other, in *A Present for a Servant-Maid : or the Sure Means of gaining Love and Esteem* (1743). Of the latter Mrs. Haywood's erudite biographer reports : " The work is a compendium of instructions for possible Pamelas, teaching them in brief how to wash, to market, to dress any sort of meat, to cook, to pickle, and to preserve their virtue. . . . One cannot expect the master's son to keep a promise of marriage without great difficulty, but the case may be different with a gentleman lodger, especially if he be old and doting. And the moral of all is : Don't sell yourselves too cheap."

In Mrs. Haywood's fiction pure and simple a similar change took place. During the fourth decade of the century she had almost seemed to give up writing it and had published nothing of the kind but *The Adventures of Eovaai, Princess of Ijaveo : A pre-Adamitical History* in one edition of 1736 and another of 1740 (where it was entitled *The Unfortunate Princess*). After 1740, however, she returns to work of this sort with a new spirit. Three novels from this time call for a moment's consideration : *The Fortunate Foundlings* (1743), *Betsy*

SAMUEL RICHARDSON

Thoughtless (1751), and *Jemmy and Jenny Jessamy* (1753). All of them excel their predecessors in construction, absence of improbabilities and lifelike character-drawing. None is pre-Adamitical or exotic, and only *The Fortunate Foundlings* concerned, like all the author's early work, with princesses and the sites where blue blood was as wantonly shed as mingled. *The Fortunate Foundlings* is an interesting novel as it marks very plainly the transition from old to new. We find in it the old impossible, pseudo-classical names for the characters, like Melanthe and Dorilaus, and the stock items of courts, nunneries, hazy campaigns, unsuspected relationships, all of which subserve involved intrigues of gallantry. But it contains also indications that life may be something more than an ingeniously interrupted sequence of love-affairs, and the heroine, Louisa, plainly owes not only the increased *concreteness*, which distinguishes her from Eovaai and her older sisters, but also much of her character and career to emulation of Pamela—though less, perhaps, to her than to Marivaux's Marianne, with whom she is exposed to the solicitation of an elderly hypocrite and made to serve in a milliner's establishment. The comparative realism of *The Fortunate Foundlings*, the sympathetic outlook of the narrator and the power of harmonizing character-description with sentiments and actions (in which particular Mrs. Haywood had, like all her tribe, been unsatisfactory before Richardson and Marivaux had shown how it was done), were carried further in *Jemmy and Jenny Jessamy*, and, notably, in *Betsy Thoughtless*—one of the most charming, as it is one of the most neglected, minor novels of the century. Like all of Mrs. Haywood's work, however, they are marred by faulty and imperspicuous construction.

THE CONSEQUENCES OF RICHARDSON

§ 5

Although the title-page of *The Fortunate Foundlings* proclaims " the whole calculated for the entertainment and improvement of both sexes " and although one half of the story perfectly accords with Richardson's ethico-artistic formula of " Harassed Virtue Triumphant," yet the moralizing vein, the didactic purpose and the altruistic ideal of mankind are absent in the last works of Mrs. Haywood and Mrs. Davys as they were from the first. Their technique they might learn to modify, but to a new angle of vision they could not, at their time of life, transport themselves. It is altogether more natural to seek for the more obvious, more essential imitations of Richardson in the writings of perfectly new authors, emulous of his peculiar fame.

Here again the women-writers come early and remain conspicuous. The first of them is Sarah Fielding, the sister of Henry Fielding and, at the same time, as we have seen, a friend of Richardson's. In her precisely those elements of the new fiction which were noted as lacking or feeble in Mrs. Haywood and Mrs. Davys are most strongly developed. Her first and most celebrated work, *The Adventures of David Simple, containing an Account of his Travels through the Cities of London and West-minster in the Search of a Real Friend* (1744), does not set out to interest the reader mainly through an intricate plot—indeed, the story in it seems more like a necessary evil than a staple attraction. What the author patently has at heart is the moral problem that her hero has set himself to solve, to wit, the discovery, by trial and error and much debate, of the assemblage of qualities most

205

desirable in a friend and, afterwards, of a human being who incorporates them. In solving this problem, Miss Fielding displayed (as was necessary) considerable talent in the apprehension and analysis of motives and feelings : to this extent and, perhaps, in the choice of her main theme, she is sentimental ; but she was endowed with a fair share of her brother's robust common-sense and a sub-acid sobriety of expression that faintly foretastes Miss Austen's. If she had possessed the ability to invent and tell an interesting story about well differentiated characters, she would have proved a strong rival to her two mentors. But her lack of interest in such essentials is shown by her next work after *David Simple*—*Familiar Letters between the Principal Characters in " David Simple " and some others* (1747)—in which she utterly gave up any idea of presenting a coherent narrative.

Curiously similar to the general history of *David Simple* is that of the second considerable embodiment (by another hand) of Richardson's own particular sentimentalism, Mrs. Frances Sheridan's *Sidney Bidulph* (1761), which was dedicated to him. Here again we find a moralizing work, not told in the epistolary way, enjoying much success at home and abroad and afterwards continued by the author in a series of letters (*Conclusions of the Memoirs of Miss Sidney Bidulph*, 1770).

" In Sidney Biddulph," the author's biographer observes, " Love was reduced to the subordinate place, and made subservient to the triumph of wedded constancy, and the exercise of the domestic duties and affections." The improbabilities attending the execution of this doctrinaire scheme are worth retailing, since their acceptance by a large public can only be explained by a wide-spread willingness to accept as practicable, nay, as potentially existing, the ideal of human nature which the sentimentalists had formulated.

The story begins where most might have ended. The hero and heroine are engaged to one another, very much in love, happy, enjoying the favour of fortune and their relatives. Into this paradise enters the sense of duty. Sidney Bidulph's mother discovers that her betrothed, Orlando Faulkland, had previously enjoyed another amour, which had made him the father of an illegitimate child. She forbids the marriage and marries her daughter to a Mr. Arnold, who makes up for his reputation as a virtuous bachelor by proving an unfaithful husband. Faulkland altruistically side-tracks the object of the wayward husband's passion, without, however, further staining his honour, and Mr. Arnold then lives respectably with Sidney till his death. Upon this event Faulkland sues for her hand, but is refused with a reminder of the duty he owes to his child's mother. The character and desirability of the lady are such, however, that virtuous Faulkland, who does as he should, sees himself compelled to kill her soon after their marriage because of the gross immorality of her life. Fleeing, he pays a last visit to Sidney and, for the third time, asks her to marry him. Grandisonian delicacy constrains her now to refuse because of the recentness of his wife's demise ! Her sense of public duty, however, is not strong enough to prevent her helping him elude the police and leave the country.

Boswell thought this a novel of great merit and was particularly pleased that Mrs. Sheridan had made no attempt, either here or in the sequel, to deal out poetic justice ; that omission, however, deprives the book of all equity, justice and balance. It illustrates the dilemma which the older school of sentimentalists in their attempt

SAMUEL RICHARDSON

to instil a strict morality by means of fiction could hardly
avoid : if they did not reward Virtue and so avoided the
censures passed on their master on that account, they
fraught it with such calamity as to render it extremely
undesirable ; and it is easy to see how precisely the dictates
of Duty and Delicacy and the persons governed by them
would be brought into disrepute by a production like
Sidney Bidulph.

§ 6

The feminine authors who succeeded Miss Fielding
and served as chief purveyors to the new circulating
libraries reproduce most faithfully the pattern drawn by
Richardson.   Especially did they perpetuate the cult of
the female " hero " and of the love-story, as well as his
doctrine that a true love-affair should give more pain than
pleasure.   Naturally, the " domestic " elements are well
represented in their work also.   The rank and file of
them did not fly so high as Miss Fielding or Mrs. Sheridan.
Their work makes quite evident their lack of all genuine,
personal opinion on art and morality, of an independent
outlook on life and of all the qualities that could interest
others in their ideas and experiences.   They are content
to reproduce with a minimum of effort one or more of the
features particularly favoured in their model or models.
Those which they were prone to single out were those
which Richardson himself would have least liked to see
isolated—the sensational incidents, in which propriety is
partially or completely outraged.   Clarinda Cathcart in
Jane Marishall's *History of Miss Clarinda Cathcart and
Miss Fanny Renton* (third edition 1767) is abducted by a
vicious nobleman ; Cornelia, the early-rising, industrious,

methodical, pious, charitable writer of edification in the novel of the same name by Mrs. Sarah Scott (1750), is carried to a metropolitan brothel by the man in whom she trusted ; the heroine of Mrs. Woodfin's *Sally Sable* (before 1764) is assaulted in bed by a rake, while a bawd helps to hold her down, but preserves her virginity, as do her sisters just mentioned. The inspiration for such incidents is not far to seek.

In contrast to these, Mrs. Scott's *History of Sir George Ellison* (1766) is meant as the biography of a man whose abundant virtues are practicable " within the common sphere of persons of fortune, in several articles within the extent of every gentleman's power," and *Millenium Hall* (1762), ascribed to the same author, is equally an educative novel. That type, all the world over, owes much to *Sir Charles Grandison*.

The epistolary form, too, was often imitated : first, it would seem (after the author of *Pamela in High Life*), by Mrs. Mary Collyer for her *Letters from Felicia to Charlotte* (?1744-9). Then follow—passing by work already mentioned—Mrs. Griffiths's *Delicate Distress* (1757), Mrs. Frances Brooke's *Lady Julia Mandeville* (1763), and three anonymous works : *Laura and Augustus* (1784), *Emily Herbert, or, Perfidy Punished* (1786), *The Twin Sisters* (1788). It should be noted, however, that the technique was found difficult by the average novelist and that the majority of them did not attempt it. *Per contra*, before the end of the century most of the outstanding novelists tried their hands at it : Smollett in *Humphry Clinker* (1771), Henry Mackenzie in *Julia de Roubigné* (1777), Fanny Burney in *Evelina* (1778), Clara Reeve in *The Two Mentors* (1783), even Jane Austen in two novels of her nonage, *Love and Friendship* and *Lady Susan*. After 1800 the technique was, in this country, only revived at long intervals.

The greater popularity of the forthright narrative-technique and of the closely related fictitious memoir, even in stories centred upon heroines and, it would seem, primarily intended for a public of women, betrays a contamination of the pure Richardsonian strain by the picaresque, realistic strain, which received new life at about the same time as its old " idealistic " counterpart. The bastardizing process, favoured by the nature of Richardson's sensational scenes, was rapid. Charlotte Summers, heroine of a novel to which she gave her own name some time before 1751, is made to declare herself " the first Begotten, of the poetical Issue, of the much celebrated Biographer of *Joseph Andrews*, and *Tom Jones*." In 1752 Charlotte Lennox put forth her *Female Quixote*. But the line of least resistance, pre-ordained to minor writers, brought most of them into the coarser groove of Smollett rather than that of Fielding or that of Cervantes. This happened even when they started out from that distant borderland between ethics and art over which Richardson had set up his lordship ; and nowhere can the process of mixture and break-up of the two old literary types be better seen than in the novel generally regarded as the finest late specimen of the Richardsonian species, Fanny Burney's *Evelina* (1778).

The staple of this book is the sentimental, troubled love-affair of the heroine with Lord Orville, a Grandison who meets his Pollexfen in Sir Clement Willoughby. It is related in a series of eighty-six letters, mostly written by the heroine to her guardian, the Reverend Arthur Villars. But by far the most vivid portions of the book are not the sentimental, but those which describe the life which a shrinking Evelina is forced to live from time to time with her grandmother, the retired barmaid, Madame Duval, and with her connections and friends. Since Fanny Burney knew Marivaux's work, Madame Duval herself may owe something to Madame Dutour ; but the heavy, grotesque " line " with which she and her surroundings are limned, the rough-and-tumble situations into which they lead one another and their reluctant guest are Smollett's and no other's ; and, as if to proclaim her kinship, Miss Burney delights to expatiate on the antics of one Mirvan, a boorish lout, whose sole delight consists in playing rough practical jokes and roaring with joy at the results—and who is a sea-captain on leave.

§ 7

The male practitioners of sentimentality in the novel, after Richardson, departed more radically from his example than the female—though one of them, Henry Mackenzie, the author of *The Man of Feeling* (1771) and *Julia de Roubigné* (1777) should perhaps be looked upon as preserving a purer tradition in his generation than Fanny Burney, to whom the apostolic succession is usually attributed. Sterne, Goldsmith and Henry Brooke, all writing in the decade of Richardson's death, show, by their wide departure from it, how individual and evanescent was the type of novel created by him and what far-reaching consequences any displacement of the balance between its elements entailed. In effecting such displacements— notably in enhancing the sensibility while diminishing the sternness of the pathos—they all carry sentimentalism from its first or puritan to its second or Shaftesburian stage.

SAMUEL RICHARDSON

Henry, Earl of Moreland, the hero of Brooke's *Fool of Quality* (1766-70), is shown ultimately in possession of those attributes of delicacy, honour, chivalry, clean living and respectfulness to the trading classes which his creator, like the creator of Sir Charles Grandison, held supreme in a gentleman. But, as the title is meant to indicate, the attributes for which The Fool of Quality is distinguished, were developed in him, not by precept and by mingling in cultivated society, by exercising perpetual vigilance over one half of his nature, but were spontaneous and untutored. Moreland is a " natural " gentleman, whose upbringing has been not unlike that recently outlined by Rousseau in his *Emile* (1762). The book, both in its general tenor and its numerous digressions, is obviously didactic and, like *Millenium Hall*, marks one channel into which the old idealistic novel was dividing, that on which William Godwin was later to embark his *Caleb Williams* (1794).

" *The Vicar of Wakefield*, considered structurally, follows the lines of the book of Job." This was William Black's grandiloquent way of indicating a debility which infects every department of this strange production (1766). The story consists of a chaotic sequence of gross improbabilities which lead to a happy conclusion and inculcate, as they are derived from, a senseless optimism, developed from sentimental premises. The gross of mankind is made to appear preponderantly benevolent, while the innumerable operations of chance tend to reward the virtuous and punish the wicked, whose unnatural machinations alone are responsible for such mischances as occur to the others. The characters are copied from approved types in fiction and comedy.

But the most formless, morally disquieting and signifi-

cant of all the later sentimental novels are those of Laurence
Sterne. In *Tristram Shandy* and *A Sentimental Journey*
(1759-67 and 1768 respectively) the cult of the tender
emotions reaches its acme. For Sterne sensibility had
become an end in itself, and the feelings from which it
wrung every scruple of satisfaction comprised varieties of
cerebro-sensual titillations at which Richardson could
only open eyes and mouth with horror : flirtations, indecent innuendos, *Schwärmerei* of all sorts (provided it
be transitory), smiling sympathy with the follies of mankind. There is no monitor within to cry " Halt ! " or
to yoke the emotions to the juggernaut of duty, no passions moving at the command of virtue, no self-discipline,
no living for others, no heroic endurance, no abysses of
hope or despair. All such things Sterne regarded as
evils, or (which amounts to the same thing) things to be
avoided, rather than as the glories of the human race, to
which we all should aspire. Between the last instalment
of *Grandison* in 1754 and the first instalment of *Tristram
Shandy* six years later, the wheel of sentimentalism had
come full circle and the " idealistic " novel—how far
from ideals it had strayed ! Richardson, surely, ends a
chapter in English literary history as definitely as he
opens one.

§ 8

In the United Kingdom enthusiasm for Richardson
and his work, probably as great as elsewhere, though, as
Scott pointed out, less extravagantly expressed, waned
somewhat abruptly at the beginning of the nineteenth
century. The taste of the times had changed from that
of his own, and rather rapidly, as we have seen. No very

vital school carried on his tradition unalloyed. But, of course, traces of his example could be found in all branches of fiction—in the distressful, high-falutin' love-stories round which shockers like *The Mysteries of Udolpho* were constructed and which Walter Scott took over from them, in the moralizing reflections scattered in the genteel novels of adventure derived from *Evelina*, in the didactic purpose of *Caleb Williams* and the like, in the domestic and predominantly feminine atmosphere of the new, ironical novel of manners created by Miss Austen.

It is characteristic of the English attitude towards Richardson that the revised and lowered valuation of his work was based mainly on moral considerations. In 1787 Anna Seward wrote that she had " always considered the Clarissa and Grandison of Richardson, as the highest efforts of genius in our language, next to Shakespeare's plays," and in 1801 she referred to the time when these two books appeared as " the brightest day of imaginative ethics that ever rose upon English literature." And in 1804 Blake wrote to William Hayley to say that " Richardson had won his heart." But the younger generation was shaking its head. Lamb deplored Lovelace's powers for ill in a passage already cited ; and Southey declared bluntly in a letter of 1812 : " My own opinion of Richardson is, that for a man of decorous life he had a most impure imagination, and that the immorality of our old drama is far less mischievous than his moral stories of Pamela and of Clarissa."

When the general public arrived at the same point of view as its leaders, Richardson naturally fell out of circulation, and a general enthusiasm for his writing was only found in isolated groups. He did not return to the mitigated favour he now enjoys until readers were in a position to ignore or leap over the gulf that separated the morality of the mid-eighteenth century from that of the mild-nineteenth. The process began with Leslie Stephen's valuable introduction to the 1883 edition of the novels and was worthily furthered by the biographies of Miss Thomson in 1900 and of Austin Dobson (a masterly production) in 1902. Clearly, however, admiration for his work to-day can only be confined to choice features in it. But those interested in psychology as a thing in itself or fascinated by that minuteness in description of sensual perceptions and in emotional analysis, which some of the geniuses of this age are seeking to develop into the "stream of consciousness novel," invented by another Richardson, will find rich rewards in studying the work of him who first set the English novel on the road that leads towards that particular goal.

<h2 style="text-align:center">§ 9</h2>

When Mrs. Calderwood of Polton was at Spa in the summer of 1756, she met there a Prussian officer, who spoke English pretty well. "He was very fond," she reports with surprise, "of reading English books ; he had read Clarissa, and thought it the finest performance ever was. All Richison's [sic] books are translated, and much admired abroad." She was indeed writing in the hey-day of the new Anglo-mania, one of the most important of cultural phenomena in the eighteenth century, of which Richardson not only shared the glories but, with his chief French translator, was one of the prime promoters.

The rise of the mania was quick. When *Pamela* appeared the Abbé Desfontaines extended a welcome to it " quoique anglois." Twenty years later, almost any

production—Mrs. Sheridan's *Sidney Bidulph*, for instance
—could be sure of favour in France, merely " *parceque
anglois* ; " and by 1748 Aaron Hill had noted that " with
due exception to deaf ears the world was never so disposed
than now, to English thought and English feeling."
This sudden popularity was mainly due in the beginning
to the (fairly literal) translation of the first part of *Pamela*
published in London in 1742. Perhaps it was principally the work of Aubert de la Chesnaye-Desbois, a
prolific hack of the time, but the Abbé Prevost was
sufficiently associated with him for the version to be
included among his collected works. Prevost certainly is
universally acknowledged as responsible for *Lettres
Angloises, ou Histoire de Miss Clarisse Harlove* (1751)
and *Nouvelles Lettres Angloises ou Histoire du Chevalier
Grandisson* (1755-6).

Richardson was inordinately lucky in his translator—
a practical man of letters, who had already published an
acknowledged masterpiece in *Manon Lescaut*, who knew
exactly what the French reading public wanted and who
also had an insatiable interest in literary novelties joined
to a selfless admiration for his discoveries that made him
exclaim of *Clarissa* : " Of all the works of the imagination,
without from motives of conceit excepting my own, there
is none that I have read with greater pleasure than this."
For the two major works Prevost recognized at once
that a literal translation would not do : what Chesterfield
called their " furieux superflu " would prove quite insup-
portable to even the most earnest frequenter of *salons*,
the crudities of style and situation would alienate a public
educated by himself, Marivaux and the younger Crébillon. His version, therefore, took the form of adaptations in the sense indicated—in *Grandison*, for instance,

Prevost claimed to have cut away five-sevenths of the
whole, and he completely re-wrote the conclusion. The
English author and continental purists like Diderot
raised objections to such treatment at the time ; but the
full and fairly literal translations which appeared beside
Prevost's would never have enjoyed any favour and
would probably never have been undertaken but for his
educative perversions.

Their success was as long-continued as immediate.
Twenty-two years after the translation of *Pamela*, Horace
Walpole could still complain of Richardson's having
"stupefied " the French people. From the chamber-
maids sneered at by Lady Mary Montagu to Voltaire, who
later sneered too, but confessed at first that *Clarissa* set
his blood a-fire, all read him and, with the vivacity of the
race, extolled him heaven-high. Baron Grimm declared
in 1753 that *Clarissa* pullulated with genius, was " perhaps the most astonishing work that ever proceeded from
the hands of man." Argenson ventured on the pro-
nouncement : " Si l'on osait, on nommerait le sieur
Grandisson un nouveau Christ apparu sur la terre, tant
il est parfait "—which has its curious counterpart two
generations later in Vigny's : " Dans le roman, un homme
parfait comme Grandisson ennuie toujours. Dans l'histoire, comme Washington, il paraît froid, et, dans la vie,
il est froidement aimé. Un homme parfait est aimé
comme Dieu, assez froidement."

§ 10

The usual consequences of popularity at that epoch
appeared in France with the same regularity as in England.

SAMUEL RICHARDSON

Of a French *Antipamela* I have already spoken ; and there are, in addition, an anonymous *Histoire de Pamela en liberté, suite de Pamela angloise* (1770) and a *Fanny ou La Nouvelle Paméla* (1767) by Baculard d'Arnaud—who set up to be a regular " English " novelist—as well as Mademoiselle Le Prince de Beaumont's *Nouvelle Clarice* (1767), a *Nouvelle Clémentine* and a *Petit Grandison*. There were produced, too, the usual adaptations, which had a greater historical importance than their English counterparts. Again, it is *Pamela* that takes the lead as model—though there were also free versions of *Clarissa* and of *Grandison*. Already in 1743 two productions revolving round Pamela Andrews appeared on the Paris stage—Louis de Boissy's *Paméla en France*, a kind of continuation at the Italiens, and Nivelle de la Chaussée's much closer dramatization, entitled plain *Pamela*, at the Française ; both failed and were jointly derided in Godard d'Aucour's *Déroute des Paméla*. In themselves these plays did little enough to help on the new and struggling dramatic species imported from England, the *comédie larmoyante*, but their model continued to work on the public for which such productions catered and may be held responsible, at least indirectly, for some of its later masterpieces. Voltaire himself went to the story of *Pamela* (as well as to its two French dramatizations) for *Nanine* (1749), that comedy of his which was put in the bill of the Comédie française on the occasion of the author's " apotheosis " (30 March, 1778) ; and his comedy of *L'Écossoise* may have incorporated a trait or two from *Pamela* also.

The second literary giant in the France of that time, Diderot, found in Richardson a spirit and a purpose much more congenial to himself than did Voltaire. His fervid

218

THE CONSEQUENCES OF RICHARDSON

admiration for the sober English domestic painter reached
its climax in that celebrated *Éloge*, contributed to *Le
Journal Étranger* of 1762 and constantly reprinted afterwards in the original or in English versions. But before
that, it had passed through the stage of emulation in his
novel *La Religieuse* (1760). In many respects, this may
be considered the " major " novel that stands closest to
Richardson's, partly for its general tone, which reveals
the same moralizing and puritan sentimentality, partly
for the salient incidents incorporated in the body of the
work. Again we have a frigid and pious heroine like
Clarissa, always acting on principle and exposing herself
to great and unknown perils rather than resign the cap-
taincy of her soul ; again that heroine tells her own story—
though her technique differs considerably from Clarissa's ;
again she is endued with a staunch female friend and
confidante ; again, like Pamela, she climbs walls, falls,
bruises herself and meditates suicide ; again we find the
now almost obligatory *clichés* of the frustrated assault in
bed and the elopement to a house of ill-fame.

These and other similar features, unnecessary to mention here, have given *La Religieuse* a bad reputation.
And indeed, it is strange, though not incomprehensible
in view of the tricks which sensibility plays on its devotees,
that so many descendants of our practical moralist should
stand convicted of indecency and immorality. Sterne
has afforded us an example from England ; in France
there was first Diderot, and later perhaps the most notorious
fin-de-siècle purveyors to " the Curious," all, either like
Restif de la Bretonne and the Marquis de Sade openly
claimed Richardson for their inspirer, or else ought to
have done so : for the Valmont of Choderlos de Laclos's
celebrated *Liaisons dangereuses*, an epistolary novel of

219

SAMUEL RICHARDSON

1784, is by universal consent directly modelled on Richardson's Lovelace.

§ 11

Among undesirables such as these Richardson, seeing eye to eye with his friend Samuel Johnson, placed his most illustrious disciple, the " very bad man " Rousseau. To Richardson's work the latter was most likely introduced by his friend Prevost ; in his celebrated *Lettre à d'Alembert sur les spectacles* (1758), soon after one footnote in praise of Pamela Andrews's critical gifts, he announced in another : " On n'a jamais fait encore, en quelque langue que ce soit, de roman égal à *Clarisse*, ni même approchant." Three years after this, in spite of his declared distrust of *belles-lettres*, Richardson's example fired him to place them at the service of Virtue and to publish *Julie ou La Nouvelle Héloïse, ou Lettres de deux Amans, habitans d'une petite ville au pied des Alpes ; Recueillies et publiées par Jean-Jacques Rousseau.*

Towards the end of *La Nouvelle Héloïse* (to give it its usual short title) we find the heroine writing to her lover and urging him to marry a friend of hers, lest he go about in spite of his passion for her, seducing the servant-girls, —which indicates a too literal acceptance of *Pamela* as a guide to life. The *motif*-hunter—after checking at Milord Bomston and his affinities with Charles Grandison —may find himself rewarded by discovering an English doctor, Mr. Eswin, practising in Italy, like Mr. Lowther of *Grandison*. But the really pervasive influence in *La Nouvelle Héloïse* is that of *Clarissa* and of *Clarissa* alone. It is to be observed in the smallest things, as, for instance, in the note which tells us that, whereas the post between Sion and Vevy now runs twice a week,

aforetime its service was but once weekly—a parallel to
the information Richardson gives us about metropolitan
church-services. But it no less than permeates the
structure and sentiment of the whole also. Both books
are written to demonstrate the improbable triumph of
strict "virtue" and to illustrate the importance of a
positive faith, together with the disastrous results which
attend the forcing of a daughter's inclination in the article
of marriage ; in both books such bare foundations are
speedily lost to sight beneath the lofty and variegated
superstructure, the luxuriant tangle of psychological
description and comment, laid upon the non-marital
love-story of the said daughter. In both stories the
tragic lovers are balanced by another pair, a light-hearted
girl, devoted to the heroine, and her heavy, loyal lover, of
whom she makes constant fun. Both stories, lastly, are
presented in the form of letters for the most part exchanged
by the four characters just indicated. In accordance,
however, with what Richardson no doubt considered
abhorrently French ideas, a *liaison* by mutual consent
between the lovers exists before the forced marriage of the
heroine.

This points the way to a much further-reaching diver-
gence between the two books. The "incessant circling
and hovering round one idea" which a truer Puritan than
Richardson, "Mark Rutherford," had to reprobate in
him, is decidedly more persistent in Rousseau : the sensuality of the characters is blatant and self-conscious and
has a definitely prurient admixture, not made any more
palatable by the demure periphrases which sentimental
delicacy required. This is, of course, a reflection of
Rousseau's own perverted nature and of his uneasy conscience which it was a vital necessity for him to pacify

by correlation to a general philosophy of life. Hence (in part) his glorification of Arcadian simplicity when male and female, unaffected by moral codes, may make love with the carelessness and innocence of butterflies and yet are somehow, magically, indisposed to promiscuity. "Nature, Nature !" he cries, "can reconcile my sensuality, my hunger for affection, my craving for virtue—and other peculiarities of my make-up, of which you may read in my *Confessions*—Nature, the absence of all inhibitions."

With Rousseau as definitely as with Sterne, sentimental literature passes from its first puritan, repressive, primarily domestic phase to the expansive, enthusiastic, "naturalistic"—and so may all but pass out of the ken of those whose attention is fixed on Richardson. And, at the same time as it does this, it joins forces with another sort of revolt against the orthodoxy of previous generations, the revolt which we may dub the "provincial," the anti-urban, the anti-polite revolt, of which Thomson is the generally acknowledged British leader. For it would be entirely unfair to Rousseau to believe that to him Nature meant nothing more than a licentious or a Shaftesburyan self-abandonment : it also meant the Lake of Geneva, its fertile and tranquil shores, the scenery of the Jura, ranging from idyllic pastures and placid sheets of water to frowning forests and deserts of inaccessible rock, the Alps of Savoy which even exaggerate these contrasts ; and *this* Nature is identified with the other Nature as the nurse of the Good, the True and the Beautiful.

§ 12

After Rousseau, as has just been said, sentimental

literature is generally referable to him as its source and inspiration, or to Sterne, and, if to Richardson at all, then mainly through one or other of them. It is interesting to the student of European culture to observe that the Englishman Richardson and Rousseau, the citizen of Geneva, both came from the Protestant borderlands lying closest to the Latin countries, borderlands which before their time had been rather importers than exporters of art and culture. It is in such countries generally that the new sentimental literature flourished most freely, declining in originality and importance as the surrounding civilization becomes rigidly Catholic in the South or further removed from the Channel and the Rhine to the North and East. From another province of this borderland, the Low Countries, come Richardson's most successful direct disciples.

Richardson quickly became known in the Netherlands, literary intercourse between those provinces and England being fairly frequent since Van Effen began in 1711 to imitate Steele and Addison, first in French and then in Dutch. When as early as 1742 an unknown translator put forth his version of the completed *Pamela* the first part had already appeared ; and the Dutch editions of *Clarissa* (1752-5) and *Grandison* (1756-7) appeared fairly soon after the originals. The last two came from the hand of Johannes Stinstra, a Mennonite pastor, with whom Richardson corresponded. It was Stinstra who communicated to Richardson the declaration of another Dutch divine, that if *Clarissa* had formed one of the canonical books of the Bible, it would have furnished proof positive of divine inspiration ! It may be noted that in Holland and, as we shall see, in Germany and Denmark—as to some extent in England—enthusiasm for Richardson seems to have been encouraged in orthodox and official circles of preachers and teachers, whereas in France and other Latin countries his fame was more usually spread by Society and by professional men of letters.

One of the Dutch parsons' wives who fell a convert to Richardson was Elizabeth (Betje) Wolff, who, many years later, met her "affinity" Agatha Deken and began a fruitful literary collaboration with her. Their joint enterprise produced, among other things, three novels : *Sara Burgerhart* (1782), *Willem Leevend* (1784-5), and *Cornelia Wildschut* (1793-6). The two authoresses were highly intelligent women of considerable reading, with a power of discrimination denied to many fiery partisans of the "old" and "new" schools at this time. Their admiration for Richardson was enormous but rational. Betje Wolff, in her Preface to the fifth part of *Willem Leevend*, dared, for instance, to speak slightingly of the demi-god Grandison ; for, after declaring that, despite some faults, the "incomparable" *Clarissa* "remains a work written for eternity" she asks whether *Grandison* can really be the work of the same man. She ventured also to assert that some of Richardson's disciples stood not very far below him—Mrs. Brooke, the author of *Julia Mandeville*, for example ; and she showed appreciation for writers whom many looked upon as arch-enemies of Richardson. In Fielding she admired the pencil of a Master and, as for Sterne, we are told that she hung his portrait between those of Rousseau and Socrates.

Many elements from the writings of all these are, of course, to be found in her and her friend's work, but its groundwork is uncompromisingly Richardsonian. From him they took the letter form, the predominant interest in the women characters, the minute descriptions of daily life, especially within doors, the susceptibility of the characters male and female to the softer emotions, the determination to instil sound moral lessons by means of their fortunes ; but, for all that, it was unnecessary for the two ladies to put " niet vertaald " (not translated) on to their title pages. Richardson may have taught them what sort of thing to look *at* and what to look out *for* : but they did not look through his eyes or behold the same scene as he did. Their work is proper to themselves and to their country : the robust sense and sharp tongue of Miss Howe is more to their taste than the lachrymose heroism of Miss Harlowe, they hold that laughter and doctrine are not incompatible, and they avoid over-emphasis and melodramatic object-lessons. In consequence they give us, especially in *Sara Burgerhart*, incomparable pictures of Dutch life in their time and scenes of a liveliness and pawky interest which do not fall so very short of Miss Austen's. With them the Dutch novel begins a continuous history much more definitely than the English novel did any time after the sixteenth century, and they stamped it in a manner still discernible to-day—in the prominence of feminine authorship, for one thing, with the concomitant domestic and intra-marital interest.

§ 13

Anglo-mania in Germany,[1] where it produced greater results than in France or the Netherlands, set in slightly later. In 1741 there appeared at Hamburg the first

[1] For the substance of this and the following paragraph I owe much to two essays of Professor L. M. Price, *On the Reception of Richardson in Germany* (*Journal of English and German Philology*, XXV) and *Richardson in the Moral Weeklies of Germany* (*Univ. of Wisconsin Studies in Lang. and Lit.* XXII.)

translation of a play by Shakespeare, and in 1743 this pioneer work was followed by a German version of the completed *Pamela*. The Preface states that the French version had already popularized the book in Germany, and indeed, there is some evidence that many of the germs of Anglo-mania were imported *via* France and the Netherlands. The German *Pamela* seems to have been the work of a syndicate of translators, some of whom were connected with " his *Britannic* Majesty's university at Göttingen." One of the chief lights of this academy, who later became its Rector Magnificus and an important person in the penumbral period of European romanticism, was the Swiss scientist Albrecht von Haller, who evinced great enthusiasm for Richardson's work and especially for the " middle-class " elements in it. He contributed a laudatory account of it and comparison with *Marianne* to the *Bibliothèque raisonnée* of Amsterdam, which appeared Englished in *The Gentleman's Magazine* for June and August 1749. He also instigated—before the appearance of either a French or a Dutch version—the translation of *Clarissa* which his colleague at Göttingen, the orientalist Michaelis, began in 1748 ; he is said to have finished it (in 1751) and to have assured a popularity for it in Germany which greatly exceeded that of *Pamela*. *Grandison*, however, did not appear at Göttingen like its predecessors, but (1754-9) at a rival seat of the Muses, Leipzig, the intellectual metropolis of Germany at that time, whose quondam dictator Gottsched hailed it as the best novel ever written. Its translation is generally held to be the work of J. F. Gellert,[1] who occupied the position

[1] Prof. Price doubts this : but at South Kensington there is a letter from a bookseller at Leipzig (? Reich), who categorically states : " Mr. Gellert, the only Man in Germany fit for such a task, sat (*sic*) about translating it."

THE CONSEQUENCES OF RICHARDSON

of Professor of Poetry and Rhetoric in the local university and has left a name as an accomplished fabulist. Gellert had warmly commended *Pamela* (for its moralizing sentimentalism mainly) and burst forth into a panegyric of Richardson, which, being in verse, is pithier than Diderot's *Éloge*, but says very much the same and contains almost as much hyperbole :

" Dies ist der schöpferische Geist,
der uns durch lehrende Gedichte
den Reiz der Tugend fühlen heisst,
der durch den Grandison selbst einem Bösewichte
den ersten Wunsch, auch fromm zu sein, entreisst.
Die Werke, die er schuf, wird keine Zeit verwüsten,
Sie sind Natur, Geschmack, Religion.
Unsterblich ist Homer, unsterblicher bei Christen
Der Britte Richardson." [1]

Gellert was the first German to seek for literary laurels where his exemplar had gained them, and his *Geschichte der schwedischen Gräfinn von G——* (1746) did for German fiction almost as much as *Sara Burgerhart* was to do for Dutch. It is a wild, disjointed sort of story, less strongly reminiscent of Richardson's novels than of *Moll Flanders*. Like the latter, it mostly takes the form of a (fictitious) memoir ; but parts of the story are duly conveyed by means of letters, and the tearfulness of many of the scenes and some super-imposed moralizing, the insistence on the voluptuousness of tears and, in especial,

[1] " This [i.e., Richardson's portrait] is the creative spirit which by means of didactic writings (poems) bids us feel the charm of virtue, who with his *Grandison* wrests from a villain his first desire to be good. Time will never destroy the works which he created : they are Nature, Taste, Religion. Homer is immortal, but still more immortal among Christians is the Briton Richardson. "

the virtuous death of Herr R's man-servant, who joyfully bequeaths his master the four hundred ducats he has saved from his liberality, seem to owe something to *Pamela*.

After the *Schwedische Gräfinn* the number of German novels is legion. At first many of them kept pretty close to the models provided by Richardson. There are free versions and abridgements of them, like *Leonore Schmidt* (1789-91), based on *Pamela*, not to mention here stage versions like *Clementina von Poretta* (1760) by Wieland, who cherished also projects for dramatizing *Clarissa* and issuing a series of letters, of an educative nature no doubt, between Sir Charles Grandison and Emily Jervois. There were plays and novels placed in England and full of "local colour," containing incidents, characters, names and sentiments culled from *Clarissa* and the two other books and often mingled with quite incongruous elements. Among the former we may mention Lessing's domestic tragedy of *Miss Sara Sampson* (1755), among the latter the *Geschichte der Miss Fanny Wilkes* (1766), which the author, J. T. Hermes, declared to be "as good as translated from the English" and which he doubtlessly hoped to sell by ingeniously suggesting in the title a compound of *Fanny Hill* and the *Essay on Woman*. Perhaps the best of the early German novels is the *Geschichte des Fräuleins von Sternheim* (1771) by Sophie von Laroche. In addition to its proper merits, it is distinguished by much to-do concerning piety, the emotions, Virtue Persecuted and Fugitive, provision for female servants ; the majority of the characters are British and a large part of the action takes place in England and Scotland.

Richardson's services, combined with those of the English macabre poets like his friend Young, were immense in loosening and bringing to the surface that fund of idealizing emotionalism which has ever afterwards proved one of the most distinctive characteristics of German art. By the time, however, that Frau von Laroche wrote *Fräulein von Sternheim* the first wave of sentimentalism had already been submerged by the second. The genius of Sterne is faintly discernible in the writings of his fellow-clergyman Hermes, that of Rousseau has left evident traces on *Fräulein von Sternheim*. Three years later sentimentalism reaches its highwater-mark in the fourth great novel of the mid-century—*Clarissa*, *Tom Jones* and *La Nouvelle Héloïse* being reckoned as the first three—*Die Leiden des jungen Werthers*, the first work of fiction by Frau von Laroche's young friend, the Frankfurt lawyer, Goethe. As *La Nouvelle Héloïse* stands to *Clarissa*, so does *Werther*, the disastrous story of a more or less virtuous love, stand to *La Nouvelle Héloïse* : to determine precisely its affinities with Richardson's work would, therefore, be otiose—and still more so those of its chief successor, Miller's *Siegwart* (1776), which stands yet another remove away.

In this second generation of sentimentalists Richardson had rather a bad name and his name was no longer invoked as by Gellert. *Pamela* is blamed for the fall of the heroine in Lenz's *Soldaten* (1776), while Richardson has villainously suggested the necessary opiate for the undoing of her spiritual sister in Wagner's *Kindermörderin* (1776). In the next generation, however, he came back to his own again : new translations appeared and old ones were re-issued, while two of the leaders of the new Romantic school in Germany, Arnim and Tieck, drew largely on *Clarissa* and to a less extent on *Grandison* for their novels of *Gräfin Dolores* (1809) and *William Lovell* (1795-6)

SAMUEL RICHARDSON

respectively—in the latter of which the influence of
Restif de la Bretonne's *Paysan Perverti* mingles with that
of Richardson !

§ 14

The fortunes of Richardson in Denmark resemble the
state of things described in Germany. Indeed, this was
an inevitable consequence of the close literary relations
between the two countries at this time. It was as a
servant of the *Danish* king that the first modern German
poet, Klopstock, applied for a diplomatic post in London,
so as to be near the author of *Clarissa*; the German
major Hohorst, who visited Richardson and Young
about New Year 1757, held the rank of captain in the
Danish grenadier guards ; and it was at Copenhagen that
the (German) *Nordische Aufseher* was published and so
reverentially debated the question " Whether in the story
of Grandison, Clementina or Harriet Byron merit the
preference." *Pamela* appeared in Danish 1743-6, translated by the would-be parson B. J. Lodde (1706-88) and
prefaced by J. P. Anchersen, who was Professor of
Rhetoric at Copenhagen and twice filled the office of
Rector Magnificus. *Pamela,* one of the very first novels
available to readers of Danish, caused the usual stir, and
we are told that the society of the Danish capital was rent
in twain between the champions of virtue (or Pamelists)
and their detractors, the anti-Pamelists ; among the latter
figured the foremost Danish writer of the time, Ludvig
Holberg, who bluntly declared in the face of the virtue-
mongers that " the portrait given of a female's charm,
[which he details,] yes, the many kisses and caresses that
are mentioned are not the material from which to derive
texts for sermons."

The usual *sequelae* of the Richardson fever followed—among them one might be singled out, a novel ascribed to the authorship of none other than Grandison himself and concerned with the fortunes of an English nobleman boasting the improbable surname of Thatlei. The later works of Richardson, however, seem to have been known to the Danish public mainly in the original, or, more probably, in the French and German versions, for it was not until 1780-2 that *Sir Carl Grandison's Historie* and 1783-8 that *Miss Clarissa Harlowe's Historie* (both translated by the lexicographer H. C. Amberg) appeared in Copenhagen.

There is nothing much to say about the fate of Richardson's books in the other Northern countries. Swedish literature seems to have missed the domestic-realistic phase of sentimentalism and to have plunged straight from classicism into *Naturschwärmerei* and the romanticism of skalds, gods, and *aesir*. Still, we know that one of the leaders in this romantic movement, Fru Nordenflycht, owned a copy of *Clarissa* and, to judge from her temperament, probably wallowed in it. Norway at this time possessed no literature separable from that of Denmark. But it is interesting to note that about 1765 there was published at Christiania Ditlevine Feddersen's Danish version of the most popular play directly suggested by Richardson—*Pamela fanciulla*.

§ 15

This comedy by Goldoni (sometimes called *Pamela nubile*) first appeared in the original Italian in 1750, the novel on which it was based having appeared at Venice in an Italian translation between 1744 and 1746 and proved

SAMUEL RICHARDSON

a great success. For dramatic purposes, Goldoni effected considerable changes in the story, for which Baretti severely rated him, notably one that cut at the very root of its epoch-making appeal. Mr. B—— becomes " Milord Bonfil," and since, as Goldoni tells us in his *Memoirs*, " a patrician of Venice who marries a commoner deprives his children of their noble rank with its privileges," the heroine's father has to declare, very believably, that his real name is not Andreuve, but that he is " le Comte d'Auspingh, Ecossois, qui dans les révolutions de ce Royaume, fut compris parmi les rebelles de la Couronne Britannique, [et] se sauva sur les montagnes de l'Angle-terre "—a detail perhaps taken from Voltaire's *L'Écossoise.* In this way, Goldoni remarks complacently, Virtue is Rewarded and Decency Preserved at the same time. Pamela and Milord Bonfil met with such applause that in the same year Goldoni had to present them on the stage again in a play dedicated to the author of *L'Écossoise* and derived, it would seem, entirely from his own inven-tion—or at any rate, from nothing he found in Richard-son. The second play was called *Pamela maritata.* Both it and, more especially, *Pamela fanciulla* enjoyed long-continued success and were adapted for the French and German stages while, in addition, the older was translated into English (1756), into Portuguese (1766,) and, as we have seen, into Danish. They suggested also further dramatizations of the story, by Chiari (1759) and Cerlone (1765) in Italian, as well as two in French.

Otherwise the vogue of Richardson in southern Europe was slight in comparison with the furore produced in France and the North. *Clarissa* was translated into Italian " for the first time " 1783-6 and *Grandison*, for all its evident attractions of partially Italian scene and personnel, not until 1784-9. Chiari, however, is said to have imitated *Clarissa* in *Francess in Italia*, and Richardson, though he did not introduce it, made the epistolary novel fashionable in Italy. Its finest representative at this time, Ugo Foscolo's *Ultime lettre di Jacopo Ortis* (1802), owes, however, more to Goethe and Rousseau than to him.

The influence of Richardson's writings on Spanish literature was almost nul. Such as it was, it apparently derived mainly from *Clarissa*, which was known in two versions adapted from the French—le Tourneur's complete version at the end of the eighteenth century and the abbreviation made by Jules Janin, translated and twice dramatized into Castilian in 1846.

After this one can glean but trifles from the field of European literature. About 1846, for instance, there appeared an opera on *Clarissa Harlowe* with French libretto by Dumanoir, Nicolaie and Guillard, which was translated into Portuguese by A. Rego (1853) as *Clara Harlowe*. The first original Hungarian novel, *Fanny hagyományai* by J. Karman (died 1795), told by means of journal and letters the story of a misalliance and of much woe and ecstasy. The contemporary firstling of Kàramzin, *Bjednaja Liza* (1792), one of the earliest pieces of fiction available to the reader of Russian, is a pathetic tale of seduction and drowning in a pond like that at B—— Hall and created a local furore not unlike that of *Pamela*. The Polish princess, Izabela Czartoryska combined with that of Rousseau and Goethe the direct influence of Richardson in her novel *Malvina, czyli domyślnŏ́śc serca* (1816).

Everywhere in the comity of European letters, from the Tagus to the Neva, from Naples to Oslo, there was the

SAMUEL RICHARDSON

stirring of new life during the last generation of the eighteenth century, a new renaissance. The countries that had shared in that of the sixteenth century defied their dictators and burst the bonds in which they had ever more rigidly confined their pristine exuberance ; many nations which had been almost unaffected before now eagerly joined in the new revival. Wherever the revolutionaries met together, they proclaimed the Rights of Man, of Genius and of the Heart, the Return to Nature and the Domestic Hearth. Rousseau was the chief among their idols ; but everywhere they were stimulated also, sometimes to emulation itself, by his master, the puritan London tradesman who had hoped he might be useful.

BIBLIOGRAPHY

I.—SEPARATE WORKS (in chronological order)

A Tour Thro' the Whole Island of Great Britain. By a Gentleman. The Second Edition. With very great Additions, Improvement, and Corrections [by Samuel Richardson]. 1738. Third Edition 1742.

Æsop's Fables, With instructive Morals and Reflection abstracted from all Part Considerations. . . . And the Life of Æsop prefixed. 1740.

Pamela ; or, Virtue Rewarded. In a Series of Familiar Letters from a Beautiful Young Damsel, to her Parents. 1740. (Continued as : *Pamela : or, Virtue Rewarded. In a Series of Familiar Letters From a Beautiful Young Damsel to her Parents : And afterwards, In her Exalted Condition, Between Her, and Persons of Figure and Quality.* 1742.) Translations : Dutch ? 1741-2 ; French 1742, German 1743, 1763 and 1772 ; Danish 1743-6 ; Italian 1744-6 ; Welsh 1818.

The Negotiations of Sir Thomas Roe, in his Embassy to the Ottoman Porte. 1740. [Dedication probably by Samuel Richardson.]

SAMUEL RICHARDSON

Letters Written To and For Particular Friends, On the most Important Occasions, Directing not only the Requisite Style and Forms to be Observed in Writing Familiar Letters : But How to Think and Act Justly and Prudently in the Common Concerns of Home Life. 1741.

Clarissa. Or, the History of a Young Lady. 1748 [for 1747-8]. Translations : German 1748-51, 1790-1 and 1790 ff ; French 1751 and 1786-7 ; Dutch 1752-5 ; Italian 1783-6 ; Danish 1783-8 ; Spanish 179 ?

Meditations collected from the Sacred Books . . . mentioned in the History of Clarissa. 1750.

The Rambler. No. 97 (Tuesday, 19 February 1751). [The remainder of the periodical is mainly by Samuel Johnson.]

The Case of Samuel Richardson, of London, Printer ; With regard to the invasion of his Property in The History of Sir Charles Grandison, before Publication. 1753.

The History of Sir Charles Grandison. In a Series of Letters Published from the Originals, By the Editor of Pamela and Clarissa. 1754 [for 1753-4]. Translations : German 1754-9 ; French 1755-6, and 1756 ; Dutch 1756-7 ; Danish 1780-2 ; Italian 1784-9 ; Spanish 1798.

An Address to the Public on the Treatment which the Editor of the History of Sir Charles Grandison has met with from certain Booksellers and Printers in Dublin. 1754.

A Collection of the Moral and Instructive Sentiments, Maxims, Cautions and Reflections contained in the Histories of Pamela, Clarissa and Sir Charles Grandison. 1755. Translation : German 1777.

(In his letter to J. Stinstra of 2 June, 1753, Richardson mentions : " A few other little things of the Pamphlet-kind . . . all with good Intention." They have not been seen. Neither has
Duties of Wives and Husbands. Six Original letters upon Duelling, in *The Literary Repository* for 1765, mentioned by Timperley, (C. H.), *Encyclopædia of Literary and Typographical Anecdote,* 1842, p. 707.)

II.—Collected Editions of the Novels

With introduction by Mangin, E., 19 vols., 1811.
   ,,   ,,   Scott, W., 3 vols., 1842 (Ballantyne's Novelists' Library.)
   ,,   ,,   Stephen, L., 12 vols., 1883.
   ,,   ,,   McKenna, E. M. M., 20 vols., 1902.
   ,,   ,,   Phelps, W. L., 19 vols., 1902.

III.—Modern Reprints of Separate Works

Familiar Letters on Important Occasions (i.e., *Letters Written To and For Particular Friends &c.*) with introduction by Downs (B. W.) 1928.

Pamela, with introduction by Saintsbury (G) n.d. (Everyman's Library.)

SAMUEL RICHARDSON

IV.—ABRIDGEMENTS AND SELECTIONS

The Paths of Virtue delineated: or, the History in Miniature of the Celebrated ' Pamela,' ' Clarissa Harlowe,' and ' Sir Charles Grandison ' familiarized and adapted to the capacities of Youth. 1756, Re-issued as : *Beauties of Richardson.* 1813. Translations : German 1765 ; Dutch 1805.

Sir Charles Grandison. Abridged : in Emmert (J. H.), *The Novelist,* Göttingen, 1792 ; and by Howitt (M), 1873 ; Oldcastle (J.), 1886 ; and Saintsbury (G.), 1895.

Clarissa. Abridged : in Emmert (J. H.), *The Novelist* Göttingen, 1793 ; and by Dallas (E. S.), 1868 ; Ward, (Miss), 1868 ; and Jones (C.H.), 1874. Also in French by Janin (J.), 1846 (Spanish translation 1846) and in German as Albertine, Richardsons Clarissen nachgebildet, 1788-9, re-issued as Clarisse in Berlin, 1797.

Pamela. Abridged : 1817 (pub. by Dick (J.), Edinburgh).

V.—CORRESPONDENCE

The Correspondence of Samuel Richardson . . . selected from the Original Manuscripts, bequeathed by him to his family. Ed. Barbauld (A. L.), 6 vols. 1804.

One hundred and fifty original letters between Dr. Edward Young and Mr. Samuel Richardson. In *Monthly Magazine* for December 1813, March, May, and December 1814, September 1815, April,

August, and November 1816, May and November
1817, April 1818.

Correspondence of Smollett and Richardson. In
Monthly Magazine for November 1819.

VI.—STUDIES OF RICHARDSON AND HIS TIMES

Boas (F. S.) *Richardson's Novels and their Influence.*
In *Essays and Studies of the English Association,* IIf
1911.

Cazamian (L.) *Richardson.* In *Cambridge History
of English Literature,* X, Cambridge University
Press, 1913.

Danielowski (E.) *Die Journale der frühen Quäker*
1921.

Danielowski (E.) *Richardsons Erster Roman.* (Berlin Dissertation.) 1917.

Digeon (A.) *Autour de Fielding.* In *Revue Germanique,*
XI. 1920.

Dobson (H. A.) *Samuel Richardson (English Men
of Letters.)* Macmillan, 1902.

Donner (J. O. E.) *Richardson in der deutschen
Romantik.* In *Zeitschrift für vergleichende Lit-
teraturgeschichte,* Neue Folge X. 1896.

Graf (Arturo) *L'anglomania e l'influsso Inglese nel
secolo XVIII.* 1911.

Köster (A), *Die deutsche Literatur der Aufklärungszeit.*
1925.

Legouis (E.) and Cazamian (L.) *Histoire de la littérature anglaise.* 1924.

McKillop (A. D.) *Richardson, Young, and the "Conjectures."* In *Modern Philology* XXII. 1924-5.

Millar (J. H.) *The Mid-Eighteenth Century.* 1902.

Poetzsche (E.) *Samuel Richardsons Belesenheit.* (Kiel Dissertation.) 1908.

Price (L. M.) *On the Reception of Richardson in Germany.* In *Journal of English and Germanic Philology,* XXV. 1926.

Prinsen (J.) *De Roman in de 18e Eeuw in West-Europa.* 1925.

Raleigh (W.) *The English Novel.* Murray, 1894.

Reade (A.L.) *Samuel Richardson and his Family Circle.* In *Notes and Queries,* 12th Series XI and XII, 1922 & 1923.

Schmidt (E.) *Richardson, Rousseau, und Goethe.* 1875.

Schroers (C.) *Ist Richardsons 'Pamela' von Marivauxs' Vie de Marianne' beeinflusst?* In *Englische Studien* XLIX, 1915-6.

Seccombe (T.) *The Age of Johnson.* Bell, 1913.

Stephen (L.) *History of English Thought in the Eighteenth Century.* Murray, 1876.

Texte (J). *J. J. Rousseau et les origines du cosmopolitisme littéraire.* 1895.

Thomson (C. L.) *Samuel Richardson : a biographical and critical study.* H. Marshall, 1900.

Thorne (W. B.) *A Famous Printer : Samuel Richardson.* In *The Library*, New Series, II. 1901.

Uhrström, (W. P.) *Studies on the Language of Samuel Richardson.* (Upsala dissertation.) 1907.

Ward (H. G.) *Richardson's Character of Lovelace.* In *Modern Language Review*, VII. 1912.

(The above is only a select list. *Cf.* also the introductions to the Collected Editions of the Novels and to the Correspondence.)

INDEX

INDEX

Carteret, John, 56
Case of Samuel Richardson,
Printer, 11, 25, 236
Castiglione, Baldassaro, 157
Cerlone, Francesco, 232
Cervantes Saavedra, Miguel
de, 196, 210
Chalmers, Alexander, 23
Chandler, Richard, 20 *f.*
Channing, J., 6
Chapone, Mrs., (sen.) 50, 81,
146
Chapone, Edward, 50
Chapone, Hester (*née* Mulso),
41 *f.*, 118
Character, Richardson's, 46 *ff.*
Charles XII, King of Sweden,
57
Charlotte Summers, 210
Chesterfield, Philip Dormer Stan-
hope, Earl of 146 *f.*, 216
Chiari, Pietro, 232 *f.*
Choderlos de Laclos, Pierre
Ambroise François, 219 *f.*
Christian Magazine, The (James
Mauclerc's), 9
Cibber, Colley, 36, 68, 124, 154,
156
Clarissa (Richardson's), 22 *f.*,
72 *ff.*, 101 *f. et passim*
Collection of the Sentiments, etc.
Richardson's) 28 *f.*, 88, 237
Collection of Voyages and Travels
(Churchill's) 10
Collier, Jeremy, 153, 167
Collier, Margaret, 42
Collins, William, 176
Collyer, Mary, 209
Congreve, William 124, 153
Conybeare, John, 10
Cooper, T., 9
Cooper's Hill, (Denham's) 55
Correspondence, Richardson's
1 *ff.*, 46 *f.*, (see also Barbauld).
Crabbe, George 199,
Crane, Stafford, 30
Crébillon, Claude Prosper Jolyot,
216
Crisp, Thomas, 162

Crowther, Sarah (*née* Richardson) 12
Czartoryska, Izabela Fortunata,
233

Daily Gazetteer, 9
Daily Journal, 9
Dance, James, 195
Danielowski, Emma, 20, 162 *f.*,
239
Davys, Mary, 159, 202 *f.*, 205
Death, Richardson's, 30, 32 *f.*
Deffand, Marie de Vuchy-Cham-
rond du, 147
Defoe, see Foe
Deken, Agatha, 224 *f.*, 227
Delany, Mary, 24, 40 *f.*, 49 *f.*
Delany, Patrick, 10, 40
Descendants, Richardson's, 12
Desfontaines, François Guyot,
215
Dewes, Mrs., 24, 50
Dickens, Charles, 3, 19, 75,
126, 174, 197 *f.*
Diderot, Denis, 218 *f.*
Digeon, Aurélien, 196
Dissertatio de Structura et Motu
Musculari (Stuart's) 14
Ditcher, Mary, (*née* Richardson)
12
Dobson, Henry Austin, 215, 240
Dostoïevsky, Fedor Mikhailo-
vich, 95
Dryden, John, 124, 198
Dufreval, J. B., 24
Dumanoir, see Pinel-Dumanoir
Duncombe, John, 42
Duncombe, Susanna (*née* High-
more) 42, 53
Duties of Wives and Husbands
(attrib. to Richardson), 237

Echlin, Lady, 27 *f.*, 146
Education, Richardson's, 6 *f.*
Edwards, Thomas, 24, 36 *ff.*,
52 *f.*, 55 *f.*
Effen, Justus van, 223

243

INDEX

Italy, Richardson and, 231 *ff.*

James, Henry, 126
Janin, Jules, 233
Jeffrey, Francis, 4
Johnson, Samuel, 23, 39,41, 47 *f.*, 57, 83, 110, 126,152, 197
Journal, the, as a literary form, 162 *f.*
Journals of the House of Commons, 9, 30
Joyce, James, 149
Karamzin, Nikolai Mikhailovich, 233
Kàrmàn, Jószef, 233
Kelly, John, 20 *f.*
Klopstock, Friedrich Gottlieb, 230

La Fayette, Marie Madeleine de, 156, 159, 161, 164
La Harpe, Jean François de, 125
Laroche, Sophie von, 228 *f.*
Lamb, Charles, 117, 214
Laura and Augustus, 209
Law, William, 153
Law Patents, 30
Leake, James, 11, 16, 22
Le Chesnaye-Desbois, Aubert de, 216
L'Enclos, Ninon de, 55, 165 n.
Lennox, Charlotte, 42, 210
Lenz, Jakob Michael Reinhold, 229
Le Prince de Beaumont, Jeanne Marie, 218
L'Estrange, Roger, 161
Le Tourneur, Pierre, 233
Letter-form of novel-writing, 90 *ff.*, 160 *f.*, 166 *f.*
Letters to and for Particular Friends, see *Familiar Letters*
Lettre sur Pamela, 65, 193
Lettres Portugaises (Marianna d'Alcoforado's), 160 *f.*, 166
Lillo, George, 155, 168, 181, 189, 198
Literature, Richardson's knowledge of, 53 *ff.*, 162 *ff.*
Lintot, Catherine, 29 *f.*
Lintot, Henry, 29 *f.*
Locke, John, 71, 150, 175 *f.*
Lodde, Berthold Johan, 230
London Spy (Ned Ward's) 8
Lyly, John, 157 *f.*
Lytton, Edward Bulwer-Lytton, Lord, 187

Mackenzie, Henry, 209
Mallet, David, 36
Malory, Thomas, 158
Manley, Mary Delariviere, 50, 159, 161, 167
Manners, Richardson as a historian of, 144 *ff.*
Marishall, Jane, 208
Marivaux, Pierre Carlet de Chamblain de, 103, 161 *f.*, 165 *f.*, 197, 204, 211, 216
Marriages, Richardson's, 7 *f.*, 11
Meditations collected from the Sacred Books (Richardson's) 22, 236
Memoirs of the Life of Lady H— 61
Memoirs of the Reign of Francis II and Charles IX of France (Castelnau's) 10
Meredith, George, 110, 118
Michaelis, Johann David, 226
Middle Class, Rise of, 150 *ff.*
Middleton, Conyers, 68
Millar, Andrew, 22, 34
Miller, Johann Martin, 229
Milton, John, 38, 55 *f.*, 181, 198
Minor Characters, Richardson's, 119 *ff.*
Monmouth, James, Duke of, 5
Montagu, Elizabeth, 41, 83, 121
Montagu, Mary Wortley, 121, 144 *ff.*, 217
Monthly Magazine, 239
Moore, Edward, 82 *f.*, 187, 20
Mulso, Edward, 42
Mulso, Hester, see Chapone

INDEX

Mulso, Mr. (*sen*) 42
Mulso, Mrs. (*sen.*) 50, 81
Mulso, Mrs. (*jun.*—*née* Prescott) 42

Murphy, Arthur 2

Murray, Fairfax 13
Musset, Alfred de 125

Nashe, Thomas 156
Nature, the cult of, 181, 199, 222, 234
Netherlands, Richardson and the, 222 *ff.*
Newton, Isaac, 1, 150, 176
Nicolaie, Louis François (*jun.*) 233
Nivelle de la Chaussée, Pierre Claude, 96, 218
Nordenflycht, Helwig Carlotta von, 231
Nordische Aufseher, Der, 230
Nouvelle Clarice, 218
Nouvelle Clémentine, 218
Novel, History of the, 155 *ff.*, 163 *ff.*, 194, 202 *ff.*, 217 *ff.*

Oliver, Rev. Mr., 68
Onslow, Arthur 36, 147
Orrery, John Boyle, Earl of, 26
Orrery, Roger Boyle, Earl of, 163
Osborn, John 15 *f.*, 21, 22
Otway, Thomas, 114

Pack, Richardson, 161
Pamela (Richardson's), 19 *ff.*, 59 *ff.*, 100 *f.*, *et passim*
Pamela en liberté, 218
Pamela's Conduct in High Life (Kelly's), 20
Pathos, Richardson's command of, 103 *ff.*, 124
Paths of Virtue delineated, 238
Penn, William, 162
Pepys, Elizabeth, 158
Petit Grandison, 218

Philips, Ambrose, 71, 102
Phillips, Richard, 3
Pilkington, Lætitia, 8
Pinel-Dumanoir, Philippe François, 233
Pinero, Arthur Wing, 112
Pitt, William (First Earl of Chatham), 150
Plain Dealer (Aaron Hill and William Bond's), 10, 54
Pluralities Indefensible, 55
Poetzsche, Erich, 54, 240
Poland, Richardson and, 233 *f.*
Politics, Richardson's, 8, 56 *f.*
Polly Honeycombe (George Colman's), 86
Pope, Alexander, 1, 35, 39, 55 *f.*, 152, 181, 199
Portland, Margaret Harley, Duchess of, 87, 146
Portugal, Richardson and, 233 *f.*
Povey, Charles, 63 *ff.*, 131
Prevost d'Exiles, Antoine Francois, 125, 216 *f.*, 220
Price, Lawrence Marsden, 225 *n.*, 226 *n.*, 240
Prior, Matthew, 152
Prompter (Aaron Hill's), 54
Provenance, Richardson's, 5 *ff.*
Psychological skill, Richardson, 125 *ff.*

Quakers, 162 *f.*, 172

Racine, Jean, 102
Radcliffe, Ann, 198, 214
Rambler (Johnson's), 23, 39, 54, 236
Rapin, Paul de Thoyras de, 77
Reade, Aleyn Lyell, 5, 240
Realism, Richardson's, 134 *ff.*
Reception of Richardson's novels, 193 *ff.*, 213 *ff.*, 215 *ff.*
Reeve, Clara, 209
Rego, Antonio, 233
Reich, Philipp Erasmus, 1 *f.*, 226 *n.*
Remarks on Clarissa, 49, 81 *ff.*

246

INDEX